SPIRIT OF '55

SPIRIT OF '55

HOW WARRINGTON WOLVES LEAPT OUT OF THE PACK

ROB WATSON

Pitch Publishing Ltd
A2 Yeoman Gate
Yeoman Way
Durrington
BN13 3QZ
Email: info@pitchpublishing.co.uk
Web: www.pitchpublishing.co.uk
First published in the UK by Pitch Publishing, 2013
Text © 2013 Rob Watson

ISBN: 9781909178564

Ebook ISBN: 9781909178342

Cover design by Brilliant Orange Creative Services.

Typesetting by Graham Hales.

Printed in Great Britain by MPG Books.

With thanks to the *Warrington Guardian* for providing the pictures for the front cover.

Contents

Chapter 1

Shattered Dreams

IT ALL ended in tears. Fans cried, players cried. It had all looked so good – won more games than any other team, scored more points, conceded fewer and finished top of the table for the first time since 1973. With a semi-final to be played at home and Saints or Wigan in the final, both of whom Warrington had beaten home and away in the two league meetings during the season, surely the 56-year wait to be champions would be over. Leeds Rhinos had other ideas. If you learn one thing from being a Warrington rugby league fan for the last 30 years or so, it would be to expect to be disappointed. So despite all the logic, none of us can claim to have been completely shocked by the outcome of that thrilling semi-final on Friday 30th September 2011.

The game deserved a better ending, a thrilling 24-24 tie being broken in the last two minutes by a penalty. Richie Myler rushed out and charged down Kevin Sinfield's drop-goal. Of course he was offside. I would venture to say that if you look at all the times in the history of the game that a drop-goal has been blocked, then the player doing the blocking had been offside the vast majority of the time. The big difference this time was that the officials actually gave the penalty in that situation, something about as frequent as an appearance from Halley's Comet. People wondered why Lee Briers hadn't gone for the drop-goal a little earlier in the game, the main reason being that Danny Buderus was in position to charge down any attempt, a position he had got himself into by being at least as offside as Myler had been. Despite Sinfield's excellent success rate throughout his goal kicking career, a rate that seems to get even better whenever a game is on the line, no doubt many Leeds fans were still nervous, hoping and praying he would manage to knock over the relatively easy kick at goal. Warrington fans would have had no such doubts, they knew with the certainty of the outcome of a James Bond tussle with a Russian henchman that Sinfield was always going to kick that goal.

Simply blaming the officials for the result is pathetically ridiculous. As with any sports match several factors dictated the outcome, perhaps the most alarming being that Warrington looked as if they had lost the ability to win close games. They may have actually suffered from their excellence throughout the season, which saw so many dominant displays and massive winning margins. The flip-side is that when it came to a match when they couldn't assert their dominance, they didn't seem to know how to win, maybe they didn't even believe they could win. It looked very much as if they had turned themselves into 'flat track bullies', through no great fault of their own. Like a dominant powerhouse of a heavyweight boxing champion, who had got used to destroying his challengers inside a few rounds. When somebody not only stands up to him, but also has great skill, the bully isn't capable of finding a way to win the fight. Warrington had become Sonny Liston and George Foreman, and for one glorious night, Leeds morphed themselves into Muhammad Ali. The fact that Warrington had chosen their challengers only served to rub a little more salt into the wound.

Warrington hadn't played close enough to their best when it mattered most. Performing at your best when it most matters is the greatest thrill for any sports person, conversely not managing it can hurt enough to bring grown men to tears. Often in sport though you have to lose something before you can win it. Many tennis players don't win their first Grand Slam final, even more golfers don't win the first time they are in contention in the final round of a major. Before Manchester United's dominance of the last 20 years, they blew a league title in spectacular style in 1992.

Two Challenge Cup successes and a League Leader's Shield in three consecutive years had understandably created a great optimism within the club. A look through the history books would tell you that optimism was misplaced. If one fact best sums up Warrington's quest to be champions, to win when it matters most, it is the fact that they finished top of the table in 1973, the last season when the champions were decided by play-offs before the reincarnation of the play-offs in 1998. Of course Warrington lost in the semi-finals of those play-offs in 1973. The following season when it was decided that whoever finishes top would be champions, and the play-offs would just be a little end-of-season tournament to generate some extra gate money for clubs. Warrington finish eighth, and yes you've guessed it, they won the play-offs.

Only three times have the Wire been champions – 1948, 1954 and 1955, one glorious, immediate post-war period, where they seemed immune from any championship 'curse'. Maybe try-scoring legend Brian Bevan was just too good to be affected by any such curse. Warrington have played in every season of top flight rugby league, making them the poster club for mediocrity.

Until the Challenge Cup wins in 2009 and the following year, mediocrity would have been just about the best compliment you could have given the club. More often than not during the wait for a major trophy between 1974 and 2009, "laughing stock" would have been more accurate. The cup wins and climbing up the league ladder have made it fun to be a Warrington fan, and even allowed us to have bragging rights over fans of more illustrious rivals. As the fans put it so eloquently: "We're not W**ky anymore." Yet still the ghost of 1955 lurks, a championship win without Bevan, Gerry Helme and Harry Bath in the team still eludes Warrington. As sporting curses go it's not quite as long as that of the Boston Red Sox, or Lancashire County Cricket Club, but it's of those proportions. The Sox finally ended the "Curse of the Bambino" by winning baseball's World Series in 2004, and Lancashire finally ended their wait since 1934 for an outright county championship in 2011. With the squad and coach at their disposal, if Warrington don't end their search for a title soon, then the club truly will start to feel cursed.

The brutal simplicity of sport means that it doesn't matter how much you 'deserve' to win anything, each sport has its own scoring system and set of rules, so whichever team or individual does best according to the criteria of that scoring system will win the contest. Whoever wins the contests that really matter will be handed the ultimate prizes. It doesn't matter how much the players, staff or fans deserve success, or which team has been waiting to be champions for the longest, only one team can be champions and that will be decided by the outcome on the pitch and nothing else.

During 1955 Sir Winston Churchill and Sir Anthony Eden were Prime Minister, Dwight Eisenhower was President of America, Rock around the Clock became the first rock and roll song to be number one in the UK, James Dean was starring in *East of Eden* and *Rebel Without a*

Cause, Jack Fleck produced one of the biggest golf upsets in history by beating Ben Hogan in a play-off to win the US Open, and American teenagers were hanging out in diners recklessly knocking back one milkshake after another. If you need any more of an idea of just how long ago it was, then picture or watch the film *Back to the Future* – that November when Marty McFly is on stage playing Johnny B Goode is the last November Warrington have been able to call themselves champions.

This book will follow the Wire for their 2012 season, as they aim to break the curse one more time. Perhaps in a summer when many in this country will be obsessed with the London Olympics and the England football team's latest spectacular piece of underperforming at a major championship, Warrington will write their own piece of sporting history. A lifetime of supporting them tells me not to get carried away with any great expectations, but then again one of the great things about sport is it allows you to get carried away on a great wave of hope and emotion. With that in mind and the continued improvement of the team's performances over the last three years, the fact that the bulk of last year's squad is still intact and that the team will be even more hungry for success after last season's disappointment my hopes are sky high, but of course I've packed a parachute just in case.

Chapter 2

The Secret

MANY OF us feel that rugby league is one of the best kept secrets in the world. We think it is a great spectator sport and we can't believe there aren't many more fans worldwide. Normally my ability to keep a secret is one thing I take great pride in, but during this chapter I will try and tell as many secrets as I can. I will start with the basics and go from there.

Like all sports it is essentially a simple game, falling into the 'invasion' category of game as each team tries to invade the other's territory. The ultimate aim is to score a try, by placing the ball down on or just over the opponents' try-line to earn your team four points, and allow one of your players the chance to kick at goal. A successful kick will tag a further two points on to your score. If your opponents concede a penalty and from the point of the penalty one of your players kicks a goal then that is also worth two points. Both those kicks described so far have to be made with a stationary ball on the floor, and over the years this has developed from players plonking the ball on the ground and giving it a whack to them slamming their heel in the ground repeatedly until they had something to rest the ball on or against, then came the little piles of sand that the player would balance the ball on. Now they all have specially made plastic kicking tees. The only other way to score a drop kick, which occurs during open play and can be attempted at any time. The player drops the ball in front of them and just as it hits the floor the player must kick the ball. If the player kicks it before it hits the ground then this is not classed as a drop kick and no points can be scored. The target for all these kicks is to get the ball over the crossbar and between the posts.

The main peculiarity of both forms of rugby compared to other sports is that the rules do not allow you to pass the ball forwards. So in order to get the ball to your opponents' try-line you must be prepared to run with the ball and to run forwards. This usually means running into a line of onrushing defenders so it's definitely a game for the brave. Defenders must halt the progress of the ball carrier by either bringing them down to the ground while still being in contact with them, or by stopping the attacker's forward momentum to such a degree that the referee shouts that the tackle is complete. Contact above the shoulders is against the rules and should be judged a high tackle.

After a tackle is complete the attacking player must be allowed to get back to their feet, then they perform a skill which is unique to rugby league, the play-the-ball. They simply have to put the ball on the ground and roll the ball back with their foot, where one of their mates will be to pick the ball up and start the next attack. Nobody is allowed to interfere with this play-the-ball process and it is a simple skill, but even at the top level it is occasionally done incorrectly. After making a tackle the defending team must retreat until they are level with the referee, around ten metres away from where the ball is being played, apart from two players who are allowed in the 'marker' position. They stand directly facing the opposition player playing the ball and the two markers must stand one behind the other.

If the defending team complete six successive tackles then it is their turn with the ball. So what tends to happen after the fifth tackle is that the attacking team kick the ball, either because if they are close to their opponents' line they think that kicking the ball gives them the best chance to score on that last play, or if they are not close to the line and they know they are going to lose the ball after the next tackle anyway they think they may as well kick the ball as far forward as they possibly can. Unlike throwing, the ball can be kicked forward but if an attacking player is ahead of the player who kicks the ball then they are not allowed to touch the ball and must be at least ten metres away from the defender when the defender first touches the ball.

If any of this seems too complicated for anyone relatively new to the sport, just keep remembering that the average IQ of a Super League squad really isn't that high, so it can't be too difficult a game to work out.

At the top level rugby league is a breathtaking display of awesome athleticism, a brilliant combination of brains and brawn, a vast array of fast-paced skills and has an intensity for every one of the 4,800 seconds of every match, which any other sport struggles to match. A common misconception is that it is merely about big men running into other big men. Essentially the game is an evasive one as ball carriers want to avoid being tackled. Of course it is rarely possible to dance through the opponents' line untouched, so if you want to play rugby league you don't just have to not mind the contact, you have to love it. To call it a contact sport is a gross understatement, it's a collision sport. Research has shown that some of the collisions in a game generate the same effect as a car crash at 50 miles an hour.

Throughout a match the attacking team are trying to be anywhere their opponents aren't, while the defending team want to be everywhere there opponents are. Every player has to defend in rugby league, one of the things that make it such a great team game. Any team is reluctant to carry even one particularly weak defender, because they know it can be difficult to hide them and that all their opponents will not only find him, but make him into a target. This can be particularly brutal if this defender is subjected to an 'assassin set', where the goal of the attacking team is to run at the same player on every play, the aim being to tire him to such an extent that he eventually misses a tackle.

Every team would love to be able to throw the ball out wide and get their speedier and classier players running with the ball in as much open space as possible. However in order to play with the style of the Harlem Globetrotters, the spadework of a navvy must first be done. This spadework mainly consists of running strongly down the middle and playing the ball as quickly as you can, to get your opponents retreating as much as possible. What goes on during and immediately after a tackle is not one of the most aesthetically pleasing aspects of the game for most fans, but what happens in those few seconds is crucial to the outcome of the game. A slow play-the-ball results in a defensive line all perfectly positioned and set to charge in again to make the next tackle. A quick play-the-ball results in a defence still retreating in an attempt to get back onside, and often they haven't had time to position themselves where they should be. If you find yourself watching a game and the team you want to win is losing and you can't really work out why they are losing, the chances are they are losing the battle of the play-the-ball, and the opposition is playing it quicker than them.

It is one of the great team games as so many different sets of skills go into making up the perfect team, but they all have to come together and the players work incredibly hard. When a team is defending they try to stay as one line, all of them side by side, leaving no big gaps anywhere. Apart from the two markers just one player is not in this line, the full-back. Generally the 13 players line up something like this when they defend:

5   4   7   12 10 9   8 13 11 6   3   2   1

Normally you are trying to make sure two little players aren't ever next to each other, allowing a big opponent to overpower them and crash through them with the ball. Also you don't want two big, slower players next to each other, in case a quick and agile runner spots the opportunity to jink in between the two of them.

In attack most teams line up something like this when the ball is around the middle of the field:

$$9$$
$$10 \qquad 8$$
$$7 \qquad 13 \qquad 6$$
$$12 \qquad\qquad 11$$
$$5 \quad 4 \qquad\qquad 1 \qquad\qquad 3 \quad 2$$

The numbers in both cases represent the number the player wears and the position that denotes. Squad numbers being introduced has confused the issue a little but here is an explanation of the positions and their roles.

1: Full-back. Their job when their team is defending is to act as the last line of defence and cover any breaks the opposition might make. They are also responsible helping the positioning of the rest of the team and any time their team is defending the full-back should be shouting at the rest of the players, telling them where they should be. When the opposition kicks the ball, it is often the full-back who fields that kick, so they need a good pair of hands and ideally they would be good at running the ball back after the kick, making some good ground and starting their team's set off on the front foot. In attack the role of the full-back can depend a little on the team they are playing for. More and more seasons pass by teams want a full-back who can join in an attack out wide on either side, to either deliver that final killer pass or to go through a gap themselves. Other teams will ask their full-back to be the main support player, so in attack their role is simply to follow the ball, then any time there is a break through the defensive line the full-back is on hand to turn that break into a try.

2: Right wingers. 5: Left wingers. Wingers are traditionally the quickest players, with the idea being that the rest of the team work to create some space for them and their pace allows them to take advantage of that space to score a try. In defence they are expected to not let the winger opposite them ever beat them one on one. The most difficult part of a winger's job in defence is judging when to rush in, leaving the man they are marking free in order to get to the ball carrier and stop the ball getting to that opposition winger. Get that right and you are guaranteed a round of applause from your fans and a pat on the back from your team-mates, get it wrong and you are guaranteed to look foolish. On the last tackle in defence, normally at least one winger will drop back and support the full-back, so they too need a safe pair of hands and the ability to run the ball back strongly. In recent times the game has required wingers to be good in the air as well as on the ground. High kicks that are trying to create a try often result in opposing wingers leaping at the same time in an effort to catch the ball and either score or save a try for their team.

3: Right centre. 4: Left centre. Probably one of the more misleading positional names as they don't belong in the centre of the field. They are just one player in from the wing and in attack their job is to supply tries for their winger and take any chances to score that come their way. This position is usually played in one of two different styles – either the player is a strong, rampaging runner who creates havoc because his runs draw so many defenders to him, or the player is more of a ball handler and passer who creates openings more subtly. In defence like the wingers they are desperate to not let their opposite number get the better of them.

6: Stand-off. 7: Scrum half. These are the two half-backs in the team, who are normally the smallest and most skilful of the 13. It is their job in attack to organise the team, making sure the others are in the best place to make the most of each set of six tackles. They also have most of the creative responsibility in the team, it being their job to link the action in the middle with the potentially destructive runners out wide. While their role is mainly one of passing the ball and getting other people to do the running, if they never run with the ball themselves they become predictable and easier to defend against, so at least on occasion they will run with the ball themselves to keep the opposition guessing if nothing else. Often the responsibility of the kicking game will fall onto the half-backs, such a vital part of the game in terms of both winning the territorial battle for their team and creating tries near the opponents' line. Some of the great half-backs through history have done little to obviously influence a game until their team gets within around 20 metres of their opponents' line and then that half-back takes charge and takes the responsibility to do the most difficult thing in the game, creating tries. In defence, because of their size they tend to be two of the weakest defenders in the team, so teams try to hide them, often between a strong second rower and centre. Half-backs know that other teams are going to try and find them and run at them as much as they can, so they should all work hard on their defence.

8 and 10: Props. These are usually the heaviest and strongest players in the team, and their job is simple. When they get the ball they are to run as strongly as they can and make as many yards as they can and then play the ball as quickly as possible. In defence it is their job to stop the opposition's props doing any of those things. It may not be the prettiest or most exciting part of the game, but countless games of rugby league have been won because one set of props has dominated the other.

9: Hooker. This is the player who touches the ball more than any other, because it is their role to get to every play-the-ball and either pass the ball from the floor to a team-mate or run with it themselves, or 'jump' out of that position with a little run and then pass to a team-mate just before being tackled. A hooker can have so much influence on the game because they can help the big strong runners gain yardage up the middle by making the passes easy to catch and run on to. Also the hooker is ultimately responsible for the direction the team takes. The half-back may be barking out instructions but it is up to the hooker to start every attack. Despite often not being much bigger than the half-backs, the hooker is expected to defend in the middle, between the two props, so hookers need to be strong defenders too.

11: Right side second row. 12: Left side second row.
These players' roles are like a mixture of those of the props
and the centres. Expected to help out the props in making
the hard yards down the middle, they are also required to be
threats out wide and capable of making breaks themselves
and passes to centres and wingers. The role suits an all-
action style of player who wants to be involved as much as
possible and loves the collisions. In defence they are often
the players that put in the biggest hits, their combination of
size and speed resulting in powerful explosions.

13: Loose forward. This is the role that probably has
the most flexibility to it in the modern game. Some teams
simply use them as an extra prop to help win that vitally
important battle down the middle. Others might use them
as an extra runner out wide to create confusion and havoc
in the opposition defence. More traditionally the role
combines the energy of a second rower with the creativity
of a half-back to produce a player who does their fair share
of hard work, but also has the skills to add to the creativity
of the side. Like the hooker they are expected to help the
props out down the middle in defence.

So that is the make-up of a rugby league team.
Numbers 1-7 are known as 'backs' and 8-13 are known
as 'forwards'. I like to think of a team being made up of
piano players and piano carriers. The more skilful players
like the half-backs, hookers, full-backs and maybe some
loose forwards and centres are the players. The props and
second-rowers are the main carriers but wingers, centres,
loose forwards and full-backs have to help out with plenty
of the carrying too. While it's easier to appreciate the
skills of the piano players, I don't care how good a pianist
you are, if you don't have someone to carry that piano
onto the stage for you then you can't play your concert.

The game is 13-a-side, but each team has four players on the substitutes' bench and these players are massively important. Each team is allowed to make ten substitutions over the course of a game and players can go off and come back on again. Usually the players who play down the middle, the forwards, are the ones who get rest periods in the game, often playing two spells of around 20 minutes with a break in between. This is because they are the ones doing most of the tackling and being tackled, the most energy-sapping aspects of the game. Substitutions both in terms of the personnel involved and the timing of the change can often be the deciding factor in a close game.

There are definitely some aspects to the game that make it an excellent antidote to the frustrations provided by the prima-donna footballers plying their trade in the Premiership. For one thing the players take the biggest of hits, sometimes completely legal, other times not so legal, and they bounce up and get on with it. A far cry from the pathetic rolling around, as if being mauled by a tiger, when an opponent has dared lay a finger on them. Then there are the more frequent occurrences of players progressing from Super League youth teams to their first team, and that you can still see local lads in the first team walking to the ground on match days. The salary cap put in place, although difficult to completely police, is at least an attempt to even the playing field and not make money the single biggest influencing factor on success.

Another thing that most fans like to see, if they are honest, is some of the fights between teams, showing passion and the fact that they are prepared to stand up for themselves and their team-mates rather than rolling around on the floor in a ridiculous attempt to get an opponent sent off. The crowd as a whole usually like it on the odd occasion when the players 'bring back the biff'. "I went to see a fight and a game of rugby league broke out," still has some truth in it, even in the modern era. Another reason to like rugby league is the way the referees speak to players and vice versa. Referees deserve a lot of credit for the way they speak to the players, knowing them all by their first names and using them. Generally they referee in a manner that shows they feel that their job is to help the players do their own job, not that they feel they are there to control the players and dictate how the game is played. Players for their part treat the officials with a great amount of respect, certainly compared to footballers. It often makes for amusing exchanges between an official and a player that can sometimes be picked up on the microphones of a televised game.

The only league in Europe that is full-time professional is the Super League, made up of 14 teams. Australia is the only other country to have a full-time professional league, which includes one team from New Zealand in the 16-team league. Only England, New Zealand and Australia are capable of fielding a truly competitive international side at the moment and if next year's World Cup is won by any other team outside those three then it will be one of the biggest upsets in sporting history, maybe the biggest. Australia are the undoubted masters of the game, always seemingly at least one step ahead of England and New Zealand in terms of producing the sheer quantity of top quality players; they also produce the majority of the best coaches. The only country to have rugby league as its national sport is Papua New Guinea.

In Europe there are two main prizes for the clubs to play for. One is the Challenge Cup, a straightforward knockout competition that culminates in a Wembley final. It is a trophy with a great history and tradition, that has maintained its prestige much better than the FA Cup has in football, still being considered a major achievement to win and only just behind the championship in terms of prestige. If you finish top of the league after all the matches have been played then you do win a trophy, but you are not champions and that trophy is regarded as being way behind the championship and the Challenge Cup. The top eight teams qualify for the play-offs at the end of the season and if you want to be crowned champions you have to win them, culminating in the Grand Final at Old Trafford.

Chapter 3

Player Profiles

WHILE I can convince myself that by writing this book I am improving the chances of Warrington winning the title, there are some men who have a lot more control over the outcome of the season: the players and their head coach. Here are the players that Tony Smith will have at his disposal for 2012.

Brett Hodgson is the first choice full-back and goal kicker, from Australia. If you saw him in the street and had to guess his profession just from looking at him, it would take you a long time to think of rugby league player. Even if you were told he was a professional sportsman, you would probably guess several other sports first. Yet as soon as you see him with ball in his hand he looks every inch a rugby league player. His relatively slight frame appears to be made of rubber, as he often gets smashed and contorted into positions that humans really shouldn't be put in, but he always seems to bounce up ready to continue with the action.

Hodgson does all the nitty-gritty duties of a full-back with a great amount of competence; the kick returns, the organisation of the defence, the cover tackling and the catching of kicks. It's when Hodgson chimes into the attacking line with ball in hand that he is at his best and has his greatest influence on the team. It is at these moments that this person who bears a striking resemblance to a character from *The Simpsons*, morphs majestically into a world-class rugby league player, as if him stepping out of a changing room with a kit on is the equivalent of Clark Kent stepping out of a telephone box in his Superman outfit.

Of all the full-backs in Super League, Hodgson is the most adept at becoming an extra half-back and acting as an extra creative player for Warrington. He doesn't always make the right decision, no one does, often his desire to be creative causes an error but I'm sure Tony Smith finds these errors easy to forgive because he knows Hodgson's creative unorthodoxy makes him a nightmare for defenders. Another great asset he brings to the team is his goal kicking expertise. Hodgson is a goal kicker, not merely a player who can kick goals. The difference between those two types of player is highlighted when they have a kick at goal late in a game to win or draw. If it's a player who kicks goals then they and the fans are hoping they will kick the goal, if it's a goal kicker then they and the fans are expecting them to kick the goal. Hodgson definitely belongs in the goal kicker category.

Chris Riley is a genuine born and bred Warringtonian, another one whose slight frame belies his profession, although he has bulked up a little since he made his debut as a 17-year-old. I believe he is most adept at playing on the wing but can always do a reliable job at full-back if Hodgson is missing. Speed is his most striking asset, but far from his only one. He is a top-class finisher, with a particularly impressive ability to pick up passes that are around his boots. Oh how he must wish that all the passes he receives are of the quality of the one he got from me during a touch rugby tournament on the hallowed turf of the Halliwell Jones Stadium. A perfectly executed angle of run drew both the centre and winger to me, a perfectly timed and delivered pass allowed Riley to scorch his way down the touchline – even though he didn't have anything on his feet other than socks. Riley plays as if he can't believe he has the honour of playing in Super League for his home town team. I hope that's an attribute he never loses and that his enthusiasm continues to rub off on other members of the squad throughout his, hopefully long, career with Warrington.

Assigning a particular position to Chris Bridge is about as easy as assigning one comical line to Peter Kay. It is easier to just say that he is an excellent all-round rugby league player. In the few years he has been at Warrington I think I have seen him play every position apart from prop. It may be that his all-round skills are most suited to a free role in the loose forward position, but it is more likely that in this Warrington team he will make most of his appearances in the centres. His evasive running, excellent footwork and great ability to time a pass make Bridge an outstanding centre. Bridge is also a reliable stand-in goal kicker any time Hodgson isn't on the pitch.

Ryan Atkins is the classic modern-day centre; powerful and big enough to play second row, and fast enough to play on the wing. Watching him over the last couple of seasons has involved an all too rare delight of watching a sports star from a team sport improve technically in some aspects of his game. His all-round handling has noticeably improved in his short time at Warrington, particularly that ability most useful to any centre of being able to catch and pass on quickly in one motion. In the 2010 play-offs when Leroy Cudjoe of Huddersfield intercepted the ball near his own line and raced the length of the field in the last minute of the game to clinch the Giants' upset win to knock Warrington out, Atkins showed he had all the spirit that fans expect from their players with a lung bursting, muscle straining chase of Cudjoe with every effort he could muster. The subsequent acknowledgement of Cudjoe's great try by tapping him on the head as soon as the try was scored also showed an impressive ability to go from ultimate competitor to ultimate sportsmanship in a split second.

If the Wire do manage to end their long wait for a championship this season, nobody would've ever dreamed up that we would have a Golden Labrador to thank, or was it a Golden Retriever? Pictures of Joel Monaghan in a compromising position with a dog were put on the internet, resulting in him feeling he had no choice but to resign from his Australian club Canberra Raiders. Putting the canine issue to one side, Warrington saw the opportunity to sign a top-class winger who is equally adept in the centres, with the added bonus being that his brother Michael was already playing for the club. While it's hardly something where you can say "we've all been there", the issue never really became much of an issue at all, with the only noticeable sign of it ever having happened being the chorus of dog noises the Wire fans greet his every try with. Last season was his first with the club and there were plenty of moments for the fans to make those noises.

Lee Briers has been Warrington's playmaker for over a dozen years, and last season he became the club's highest ever point scorer. Up until the last three seasons he had been with the club through thin and thin. There has never been any doubting his rugby league skills, and at any point in his Warrington career he has been capable of controlling any game and cajoling his team to a win that they couldn't have achieved without him. What there had been doubts about was whether he was making the most of his skills and whether his attitude matched his aptitude. His off-field antics were far from being as impressive as his on-pitch ability.

During the reigns of previous coaches, fans got the impression that Briers had a big say in the running of the team and that he was also given more leeway than other players, particularly regarding those off-field antics. When Tony Smith came along one of the first decisions he made was to drop Briers from the team. It definitely seems to have had the desired effect. It is to Smith's great credit that he had the courage of his convictions to make such a bold decision, and it is to Briers' great credit that he responded to it in the manner that he did. The last three years have been Briers' most consistently good performances in his whole time here, and a lot of that has been because he now seems to understand that he can have the best possible effect on the team's performance if he does try to get involved in virtually every attacking play.

Of course this has been made easier by the fact that the rest of the team are the best players Briers has played with during his time at the club. As creative a half-back and playmaker as there has been at any club in the Super League era, he is capable of breaking down any defence with one of his vast array of passes, a dummy or a pinpoint accurate kick. His understanding of the game is also better than the vast majority of other players, which along with his eye for the unorthodox combine with his skills to make all that creativity. The fact that he is the Warrington player that opposition fans most love to hate is an excellent assessment of how good a player he is and how important he has been to the Wire over the years.

Richie Myler was brought in after the 2009 season to add to the half-back options for the Challenge Cup winning squad. Despite being only 22 he has already made several appearances for England. While that is partly a reflection on the lack of dominant English half-backs, it is also because of Myler's understanding of the role of a half-back, his organisational skills and his infectious enthusiasm. Of all the qualities he brings to a rugby league team, it is his support play that is the most outstanding. You would be hard pushed to find a better support player anywhere. That is one of those skills of the game that looks so easy; following the man with the ball, how hard can that be? Yet in the history of the game only a chosen few in each generation have proved themselves to be masters of the art. If not already there Myler is well on his way to being one of this generation's masters.

Adrian Morley is the sort of leader who wouldn't have to ask you to go over the top, leave the trenches and charge out into no man's land, he's the sort that would make you want to follow him up the trench ladder. Definitely one of those players that you would always rather have in your team than against you, if only for the fact that you wouldn't have the prospect of being hit by one of his trademark bone-shuddering tackles and of trying to halt one of his powerful runs. You don't get to be the most capped player in your country's history without being exceptional. Australian clubs don't sign too many British players. The fact that not only was Morley signed by Sydney Roosters, but that he had a long, successful career over there is another, impossible to ignore, sign of his quality. His sheer physical presence seems to lift any side he plays for. He leads the defensive line, never letting them lose the required speed, and any time there is some serious donkey work to do carrying the ball away from his own team's line, Morley is always happy to put his hand up.

The fact that Michael Monaghan's switch to hooker came at the start of Warrington's excellent run from partway through the 2009 season onwards is far from a coincidence. A strong case can be made for Monaghan being Warrington's most important and influential player. He has that subtle ability to pass the ball in such a way that can help the players running off him to take the team forward. Another of his great abilities is knowing when to set off on a darting run himself; sometimes only a few steps are required to attract defenders to him and put another player through a gap with a quick pass. That Warrington are always a threat to score from anywhere on the park is largely down to his quick thinking, opportunism and positive mindset. Once Warrington get close to the line he is still a massive threat, good decision making and the ability to fling out long, accurate passes make him the ideal hooker to have when your team is in the 'scoring zone.'

Gareth Carvell is one of those players that are getting ever rarer in the sport of rugby league, in that by taking one look at him you can confidently guess what position he plays. That position is prop and not many play it better than Carvell. His strong runs usually take at least three players to halt his progress, often more. Like most of the Warrington players he is adept at offloading the ball while being tackled, often when it barely looks possible. Not a player who is likely to dazzle onlookers with his skills, but one that all the players will be most grateful is on their team.

Over the last few years Ben Westwood has become firmly established as a fan favourite. This has come about because of his complete disregard for his own personal safety as he flies into tackles, often producing the biggest hit of the match. The other attribute the fans love so much is his excellent work-rate, always putting his hand up to run the ball in tough situations. He has been at the club for ten years now, but it's only since his conversion from a centre to a second rower that he has become a terrace favourite. Even his most ardent fan must acknowledge that for someone who passes the ball about as frequently as a leap year occurs, playing centre was never going to be his best position. That is like expecting a thoroughbred shire horse to win The Derby. Now he is a square peg in a square hole, Westwood is one of Warrington's most important players. It's strange to think that the signing of Martin Gleeson might have actually had such a positive effect on the club in the long term. Gleeson was a world-class centre but had plenty of problems off the field and didn't seem to do a great deal for team spirit at Warrington. At the time we signed him our centres were Toa Kohe Love, an extravagantly talented Kiwi, and Westwood. It was the signing of Gleeson that prompted the move of Westwood into the second row.

Trent Waterhouse was the biggest name of the newcomers for this season. Anybody who has been chosen to represent Australia can obviously play the game of rugby league exceptionally well. Waterhouse is tall and powerfully built in the classic mode of a prototype second row forward and it is very difficult to imagine him playing in any other position. His willingness to offload the ball should help him fit in with the style of play of the team, while his class and experience should definitely help make him an asset to the club.

Ben Harrison is a Cumbrian lad, but has been at the club since his mid-teens so is very much a product of the youth system. A phenomenal work-rate and an ability to produce several hard tackles in a game are his two most noticeable qualities. He is another one of those players that lacks in dazzling skills, but more than makes up for that with his work-rate and strong defence. He does lots of the 'donkey' work, like putting pressure on opposition kickers as well as sharing the workload for those tough runs with the likes of Morley and Westwood.

Mickey Higham would be the first-choice hooker at a lot of Super League clubs, but at Warrington he is very much the deputy to Michael Monaghan – an excellent deputy to have. He is at his best when defences are slightly out of position or tiring and he can take advantage with his darting runs from behind the play-the-ball. Higham plays the most important role of a hooker very well, that being getting his team going forward down the middle of the pitch. Just like Monaghan he is also more than solid in defence.

Simon Grix is from a similar mould to Chris Bridge in that he is an extremely versatile rugby league player, able to play well in several positions. Personally I feel his all-round abilities are best suited to playing in the back row, either second row or loose forward. Grix is always reliable in defence and can make several breaks in attack, especially after using his excellent hand off and freakish ability to be able to wriggle out of tackles.

Paul Wood has been at the club for over ten years and has turned in few poor performances in that time. He doesn't look to be the biggest of props, but he never gets bullied and rarely gets smashed or dragged backwards. This is mainly due to two things, his excellent footwork and his toughness. Wood is also never going to be classed as one of the stars of the team, but he is a vital asset to the squad.

Stefan Ratchford and Chris Hill are the other close-season signings, both added partly on potential rather than being classed as the finished product already. Ratchford was signed from Salford, where he spent most of his time as a half-back, but he is another player who can fill in various positions when required. Hill's job description will be far more simple, that being to play prop forward, to run hard with the ball and tackle hard. He certainly did that last year for Leigh, but that was in the league below Super League. If he can make the step up then he could be a very useful addition to the pack.

At some point in the season it should feel like the Wolves have made another signing, that being when David Solomona returns to action after breaking his leg in pre-season. He never looks like the fittest of players, but his power production is immense, often taking three or four players to bring him to a halt. His most eye-catching ability though is to offload the ball from seemingly impossible situations.

As well as those established players, there are several young players who will be looking to make an impact on the season. Cooper, Blythe, Williams and McCarthy will be looking to make the step up from making occasional appearances to being established first-teamers. Below them, even younger players like O'Brien and Evans will be hoping this is the season they break into the first team and make a real impact.

If these player profiles are anything to go by then unless another Super League team make an audacious triple transfer swoop for Superman, the Incredible Hulk and Captain America then the Wire will surely win the championship.

Chapter 4

Match Reports

Round 1 v Hull (away) – 5th February 2012

AFTER A winter of wondering what might have been and just how Leeds managed to beat us in that semi-final, it was finally time for Warrington fans to focus on the new season. Watching Challenge Cup finals from 2009 and 2010 on DVD, along with the wins over Wigan in the 2009 semi-final and the penultimate league game of last season, a game that went a long way to clinching our first League Leader's Shield since 1973, could at long last be replaced by live action. A new chapter in the club's history is about to be written, new heroes to be made and maybe a few villains, new stories to be told and another rollercoaster ride to go on.

Since the sport switched to a summer season, it always seems a little odd that every campaign starts with winter usually still in full flow, and finishes with winter well and truly on its way again. As opening fixtures go this is a tough one, without playing one of the teams expected to be the main title rivals. Hull are one of those clubs you could describe as being in the second tier of Super League challengers, unlikely to finish in the top four but equally unlikely to finish outside the top eight. For a few years Hull had been bracketed alongside teams like

Warrington and Huddersfield as those being most likely to break the stranglehold of the 'Big Four' of Leeds, St Helens, Bradford and Wigan. For a few years they were actually a good club for Wire to model themselves on, and despite not being part of the game's elite four, they managed a Challenge Cup win in 2005 and a Grand Final appearance a year later. Wire fans would be left thinking that if Hull can do that, then why can't we?

Hull is a genuine, traditional rugby league city, the sort of place so obsessed with the sport you think it might be the only place where they knock down supermarkets to build rugby league pitches. There are some great derbies in Super League like Wigan v St Helens, Leeds v Bradford, Warrington v Widnes and Castleford v Wakefield. But it is hard to argue that any of them have more passion and a more intense rivalry than Hull v Hull KR. Technically it is the only Super League derby as sports historians will tell you that a derby is a match between two teams from the same city or town. The fact that Hull is the only city that has two Super League teams is a great indication of how much rugby league means in Hull.

The first game of the season is always a difficult one to go into with any great optimism or pessimism. Pre-season friendlies are never that great a guide to the quality and form of a side. There are often a few strange results in the first month or so of the season, mainly because some teams hit the ground running a lot more than others, in terms of fitness levels, sharpness and timing. With the reintroduction of the play-offs to decide the champions the emphasis is taken off the early season results. A team can afford to have a bad start and still turn out to be dominant champions in October. Obviously you would rather your team win the first few games than lose them, but as much as anything you're looking out for how your team is shaping up in terms of new signings settling in, any positional changes for players and how the team spirit looks.

Warrington make one of the longest trips they will make all year, with a few youngsters in the team. After going behind to a Kirk Yeaman try, new signing Trent Waterhouse scores Warrington's first try of the season. A tight game ensues where neither side is ever more than six points ahead. With a couple of minutes left Wire find themselves four points behind. A surging break down the right-hand side results in teenager Rhys Evans going over in the corner for the equalising score. Ben Westwood is deputising as goal kicker for the injured Brett Hodgson and unfortunately cannot make the winning goal from the touchline.

A draw is a rare result in rugby league, so you never really consider it as an option in advance of a game. Given the standard of the opponent, playing on their home ground, it being the first game of the season, that they had a few first-team regulars missing and that they were four points down with two minutes to go then in this case a draw isn't too bad a result at all for Warrington.

Final score: Hull 20 Wire 20

Round 2 v London (home) – 12th February 2012

DESPITE NEVER having won the championship or the Challenge Cup, London are one of the most talked-about teams among rugby league fans. The great debate is about whether they belong in Super League. Traditionalists will argue that their history as a club and the lack of history of amateur rugby league in the city means they shouldn't take their place among the game's elite. Number crunchers will point to poor attendances and financial difficulties as evidence that they don't belong. Expansionists and dreamers who want to see the game stretch its boundaries will defend London's right to be in Super League. Personally I'm happy for them to be in there, as long as they continue to do the work I believe they have been doing over the last few years in the local community, developing young players and amateur clubs.

Whether we like it or not, London is by far the biggest and most dominant city in England, and if we can establish rugby league there to any decent degree then it can only help our game. One of the many chips we have on our shoulders is the lack of national press coverage for our game. A lot of national press is in London and if they have a local team to write about in the long term that can only be a good thing. It is a shame and a constant cause of frustration for the game, that in a city of eight million people they can barely mange to get four thousand watching their home games. Maybe if they continue to develop local players it will help make it easier to market the team to a paying public.

Standing behind the sticks in the West Stand gave me a great view of the filled-in corners, the seated corner in particular looking fantastic. The team had got off to a so-so start on the road at Hull the week before, and now we were waiting to see what sort of start they would make at home. Two new players to cast an eye on; Waterhouse looks every inch the classy powerhouse he's been regarded as in Australia for years and Ratchford looks to be from a similar mould to Bridge and Grix, an all-round rugby league player, capable of filling in for us in several positions.

Overall the team made several mistakes, far too many dropped balls, sloppy offloads and bad decisions – and I loved it. It is great to see a professional sport team in the modern era that seem aware of their duty to entertain the fans who pay their wages. Any more entertaining than this and they will have to start wearing longer shorts, sleeveless tops, enter the field to the tune of Sweet Georgia Brown and have it in their contracts that the opposition must play along with the entertainment and ultimately lose.

Before handing over my £20 to get in I did wonder whether I could spend that more wisely elsewhere but the long-range tries that Ratchford and Atkins scored with help from Evans and Briers respectively were easily worth a tenner each. The flick pass for Monaghan's second try must have been part of a buy-two-get-one-free deal. Of course it's frustrating when the ball goes to ground so often, but if you want a rainbow, you have to put up with the rain. I'm sure the players know they will probably have to play better to beat the other top teams, but they also know that they are capable of scoring many tries against anybody from anywhere. I for one am looking forward to my next opportunity to watch them.

Equally pleasing as all the entertainment is the spirit the team play with. Never once after any of the numerous errors was the offending player shunned by his team-mates, instead they encourage him and assure him that they will all do their best to make up for his mistake.

They have turned the *Spirit of '55* into a believer, so here's hoping they keep believing all the way to victory at Old Trafford.

Final score: Wire 50 London 10

Round 3 v Huddersfield (away) – 18th February 2012

HUDDERSFIELD IS known as the home of rugby league, a reference to an historic meeting in 1895 that took place in the George Hotel. It is surrounded by the heartlands of the game and is considered part of those heartlands which makes their crowds being of a similar level to London's so disappointing, especially over the last few years as they have had an exceptional side, who have come close to winning trophies. Those fans who do turn up have built a great rapport with Wire fans in general over the last few years, starting probably from their shared day out at Wembley back in 2009, when both clubs were looking to end a long wait for a trophy after they had broken the stranglehold of the established big clubs. It is a legendary club, with a great history, but like its football team, their trophy-winning halcyon days came before the Second World War.

If last week was all about the beauty, this win was all about the beast. Of course there were some excellent tries scored, with brilliantly impressive handling skills, but this particular win was about much more than that. Mental and physical toughness were put to the test by a good and tough Huddersfield side. Two injuries early on, first to Grix and then to Harrison, who had replaced him at loose forward, meant the playing resources were stretched to the limit, with Morley and Michael Monaghan in particular playing more minutes than was probably in the original game plan. For some Warrington teams of years gone by, that in itself would have been enough to leave them settling for a defeat. This team already look to have a determination about them, a determination that will not allow them to accept defeat until the final whistle has blown and they are behind on the scoreboard.

A high shot was delivered to Briers' jaw that looked more like Bruce Lee than Tommy Lee. This seemed to be the catalyst for an angry start to the second half, Chris Bridge in particular looking to be struggling to ward off the red mist. Without condoning violence it is always good to see your team willing to stand up for each other in any physical confrontation, and on a few occasions Wire showed they were prepared to bring back the biff to stand up for a mate.

Finding that balance between sufficient aggression to play a collision sport, and the composure to impact positively on the scoreboard, Wire gradually took control of the second half and were worthy winners. Although it was scrappy I was particularly pleased with the last try. Ratchford's and Myler's reaction to the ball hitting the floor and the lack of a whistle that the Huddersfield players were waiting for was the sort of reaction that is a coach's dream. Playing to the whistle is drummed into every young player from an almost embryonic age, yet is often forgotten when it matters most by elite level performers. The ball hitting the ground causes so many tries in rugby league it's amazing, all because one or two players react when others don't.

Overall the most pleasing thing about this win was that it was a close one. The only criticism that could be levelled at the team last season was that they had seemed to have lost the ability to win a close game, either they dominated their opponents, or they were squeezed out in a close one. Hopefully this is another sign that the team are finally ready to follow in the footsteps from 1955.

Final score: Huddersfield 22 Wire 32

Round 4 v Hull KR (home) – 26th February 2012

IN THE Super League era Hull Kingston Rovers have definitely been the poor relation of the two Hull clubs. With regards to trophies won in their history they are a match for their city rivals, but when Super League was being created in 1996 Hull KR were in the wilderness, in all sorts of financial trouble and a shadow of their former self. They didn't make their way in to Super League until 2007. Since then they have been more than competitive, making a few play-off appearances, but never looking like landing any of the three trophies available. It seems they have hit those financial troubles again. Maybe Hull is only big enough to support one Super League team, but it would be a shame to lose one of the traditional clubs from Super League in a city that is so entrenched in the sport.

The most impressive thing about this performance was Wire's defence, particularly when close to their line, playing against a team that had scored 36 points against Saints the previous week. You could see how Hull KR could score so many points – plenty of runners out wide making sure the defence has to make a lot of good decisions, well marshalled as always by Dobson. Yet despite several drop outs and KR starting plenty of other sets in Warrington's half, the Wire only conceded two tries, both of which were extremely well worked. The defence looks extremely well organised, but at least 90 per cent of defence is about desire and attitude and it's pleasing to see just how much pride this team has in their defence.

This great desire and ability to defend allows Wire the freedom to play their expressive style with ball in hand. Playing that expansively and producing that many offloads is always going to result in some handling errors, some well inside your own half of the field. Some Warrington teams of the pre-Smith era played almost as expansively, but any time they produced a handling error close to their line, you got the feeling they expected it to result in a try, and of course that meant it often did. By great contrast after every error made by this team the player 'guilty' of making the error acknowledges his mistake, the players nearby give him a consoling pat on the back and the fingers go up pointing to the sky, signalling that the team now needs one minute of effort on defence to see out that one set of six tackles and make up for that minor digression.

Again there were plenty of groans and criticism from fans any time an offload didn't go to hand and resulted in giving up possession. Again there were some magnificent tries scored and some majestic handling moves. In any sport there should be one question in the mind of a player at all times, that being: "What would the opposition least like?" I think that a lot of the time this Warrington team is doing what their opponents least want them to do, and every handling error they produce is a great source of relief for the opposing defence.

The fans cheer when a flowing move, consisting of a mix of fast passes and offloads, results in a thrilling try, they moan when the ball is lost, but must acknowledge it's difficult to have one without the other. If you decide to eliminate the errors, you're eliminating the tries too. It could be argued that tries would come anyway from a gradual build up in pressure, though I would argue not as many. But I for one wouldn't want to pay my 20 quid to watch tries scored by gradually building pressure, I'm far happier paying to watch a team that could score at any time, from any point. They will score from kick-offs, from scrums near their own line, they will score when their opponents drop the ball – when any other team would just drop on the ball, they will score!

Final score: Wire 42 Hull KR 10

Chapter 5

History of Rugby League

RUGBY LEAGUE is a rare sport in that it can pinpoint the exact day of its origins. It was at the George Hotel in Huddersfield, on 29th August 1895, when the outcome of a meeting was that 22 rugby clubs decided to split from the RFU and create their own 'Northern Union'. The simple reason for the split was that factory workers in the north wanted payment for playing rugby on a Saturday, to make up for wages lost from taking time off from work. Any sort of payment was strictly against the amateur ethos of the southern-based RFU. Old Etonians wouldn't dream of doing anything as vulgar as accepting money for playing a game, the thought of which probably caused many of them to choke on their cucumber sandwiches and Pimm's.

From that bold breakaway moment the Rugby Football League (RFL), as it became known in 1922, has continued to be innovative with many aspects of its sport. Rugby union often follows suit, but usually long enough afterwards to create the impression of thinking for themselves. In the case of open professionalism they hung on for the best part of 100 years. A ten-minute sin bin for certain fouls, video referees, end of season play-offs and having leagues rather than merely playing friendlies have all found their way into rugby union, long after being initiated in league. Now they are talking about switching to a summer season. Maybe it's just a matter of time before they have a klaxon to signal the end of each half to the referee, lose a couple of players from each team, scrap lineouts, replace rucks and mauls with a play-the-ball and change the scoring system.

As for the invention of rugby in the first place that is most commonly traced back to the story of William Webb Ellis, a public schoolboy at Rugby School, who during a game of football in school time picked the ball up and ran with it. Waving away what presumably was a chorus of appeals for handball, the school masters instead thought that this was a great opportunity to start a new game. So the early days of rugby had many similarities with football, like the idea of scoring more goals than the opposition, with a goal at each end. Indeed when it first started the teams would simply count how many goals they scored to determine the winner, just as in football. Placing the ball down on or just over the opponents' try-line wouldn't score you any points in itself but it would allow you to have an attempt at goal, or to put it another way a 'try' at goal, hence the name. The game spread around the country quickly and almost as much as football, then came the split in 1895 and the two codes have been too busy fighting each other ever since to notice that football has swamped them both.

Those roots of rugby league have meant that it has always been known as a working-class game, something most if not all fans are proud of and keen to keep even in the modern world. To this day most arguments between fans of league and union won't last for long without references to flat caps, whippets, factory workers, stuck-up toffs and southern softies. Rugby league fans tend to wear it as something of a badge of honour, showing they are proud of their working-class heritage.

In contrast to its innovative ways of changing the sport, rugby league's glaring weakness has been its inability to spread the popularity of the game away from the areas those 22 clubs occupied in 1895. Even in the modern, highly professional stage the sport is now in, you could visit all the strong, established clubs without going much more than ten miles off the M62 motorway. Some towns like Castleford and Widnes would barely register on any sort of national consciousness if it wasn't for their rugby league teams.

Warrington have never been out of the top flight, but if the Swedes hadn't built a shop there even people in the north-west, who weren't rugby league fans, would probably only think of Warrington as somewhere you went past on your way between Manchester and Liverpool. Maybe now, with back-to-back Challenge Cup wins, people will know of Warrington for something other than self-assembly furniture and a motorway network. Both Hull and Wigan have spent time in football's Premiership recently, yet still most people think first of rugby league when those names are mentioned.

In recent times the RFL have shown a keenness to spread the game away from its traditional areas, at times at the expense of some great old rugby league teams and towns. They have parachuted teams into Super League, basing them in Paris, Gateshead and South Wales, all of which failed to take root and be a success. Eventually they realised that basing a French rugby league team in Paris would be like basing an English croquet team in Hull. Since they tried again in France, basing a team in the rugby league strong hold of Perpignan, the venture has been much more successful.

After two years in Super League in 2009 and 2010, the Celtic Crusaders moved from their base in South Wales up to Wrexham. They left behind them a developmental team for Welsh-based players to play in the Co-operative Championship 1 (two divisions below Super League). Had the RFL come up with this plan originally people might have said it was a brilliantly clever one. Basing the Super League team close to the heartlands, so that away fans can travel to it easily, and new fans could be attracted from the many rugby league fans in nearby areas like Cheshire and Merseyside, but still having the franchise in Wales, while at the same time allowing the game in the south of Wales to develop from a more grassroots level. Instead the way it came about looked more like some sort of a retreat, causing some embarrassment to the game as a whole. The end result looked like a plan as cunning as a fox who has just been appointed as professor of cunning at Oxford University, the original plan having far too much of 'Baldrick' about it. As it turned out the club could only manage one year up in Wrexham, before admitting defeat and relinquishing their Super League status because of financial reasons.

Many things have hindered the spreading of the game on an international and national scale, most particularly the banning of the sport in the armed forces for many years and the great reluctance of many high schools to play it. But on the issue of stretching its boundaries the game has to acknowledge that its greatest enemy has been the game itself. At the end of this season eight of the top nine clubs would be ones who were part of that original breakaway of 22 teams back in 1895. That's either reassuringly traditional, or a spectacular lack of progress.

Warrington have been around for every season since that 1895 split. It is a record to be proud of that they have never been out of the top flight. It is difficult to think of another British sports team that is more commonly known by its nickname by people within the game than Warrington being known as "Wire". The reason for the nickname is that producing wire was the main industry of Warrington for several years. It is a nickname that has survived strongly into the modern era of official, marketing-led nicknames. Personally I like the old and the new, I love the tradition of still referring to us as "The Wire", but I also think the mascot wouldn't have been quite as successful at bringing on board several new young fans if it had been a piece of wire rather than the loveable, fluffy Wolfie.

Chapter 6

Broken Sporting Curses – Boston Red Sox

WARRINGTON ARE far from alone in being a sports team that have suffered a long wait to win a championship. Several clubs in many sports have felt that they were cursed. With team sports the wait can be stretched out over so much longer than in the case of an individual. Every summer from around 1996, for about ten years, the British public would look forward to Wimbledon that little bit more than they had done for years, because there was genuine hope that Tim Henman could win the men's singles title. That hope never quite became expectation and certainly never became reality. At the time it did seem like a long time, but compared to team sports that have been around for over 100 years an individual chasing a dream for ten years is barely more than a blinking of an eye. Also when the individual retires, whether successful or not, the wait is over, because fans know the player cannot possibly win it anymore.

Another slight oddity when it comes to sporting 'curses' is that rather than clubs who have never won the title, it is those that haven't won one for a long time that seem to feel the weight of history more, as if they are trying to emulate their predecessors at the club, who have shown it is possible for that club to be champions. Fans' expectations of current players do tend to be shaped somewhat by the exploits of previous players. If they hadn't seen such riches, they could live with being poor.

Possibly the most famous curse in sport is the "Curse of the Bambino" that was supposed to be to blame for the baseball team Boston Red Sox for not winning the World Series since 1918. The story behind the curse begins when they sold their star player Babe Ruth to their arch rivals New York Yankees. By 1918 the Red Sox were the dominant team, having won four out of the previous seven World Series, while the Yankees were yet to register their first series win. At the end of the 1919 the Red Sox owner sold Ruth to the Yankees, to raise funds to put on a Broadway show. In the following 84 years, the Red Sox couldn't muster up another series win, while the Yankees racked up 23 wins. To make matters worse for the long-suffering Red Sox fans, the format of the competition meant that the Red Sox would often have to beat the Yankees in their quest to win the big one, and it was often the Yankees themselves that ended Boston's dreams for another year.

Books have been written about the subject including *Breaking the Curse* and *Faithful* – a fans' eye view on the 2004 season as two fans, one of them horror writer Stephen King, tell the story of the season through their journal entries and correspondence between each other. Films have been made about it, including *The Perfect Catch*, an American version of *Fever Pitch*. The whole situation has been used as a metaphor as people apply their own theory on Boston's inability to win when it counts most and apply it to other situations in life. This curse was introduced to a whole new audience when it featured in the smash hit television series *LOST*. The father of one of the lead characters would often tell him "that's why the Red Sox will never win the series", a reference to some things being meant to be and decided by fate.

Finally in 2004 the curse was ended and in the most dramatic and history-defying way imaginable. If someone had written the story it would never have seen the light of day for being too unrealistic. In what we would simply call a semi-final, the Red Sox were once again up against the Yankees, in a best of seven match series. After losing the first three matches, a freaky play in the fourth game led to a victory and they went on to become the first team to ever come from three matches down to win a seven-match series, leaving the Yankees and the rest of America stunned.

Still they hadn't won the World Series yet and most people were still expecting them to somehow blow it again when they came up against St Louis in the World Series match, despite their heroic comeback against the 'Evil Empire'. Clearly this particular bunch of individuals were either too mentally strong or simply too good at baseball to be affected by any curse, and they stretched their winning run to eight games to sweep the series 4-0 and well and truly end the curse. The character in *LOST* was busy being lost on a mysterious island while all this was going on, and another character shows him the footage of the series win to show to him that he does have control over his own destiny and fate can be fought.

The phrase "Curse of the Bambino" was only coined by writer Dan Shaughnessy in his book of the same name, published in 1990. It wasn't until then that Red Sox fans had something to call their pain. Bizarrely enough the World Series winners the following year were the Chicago White Sox, who had waited since 1917 for a World Series win, one year before the previous Red Sox success. In 1919 eight Chicago players were convicted of accepting bribes to throw the World Series match. Maybe "Curse of the Bribes" didn't quite have the same ring to it. For whatever reason the story behind the Chicago's even longer wait for a World Series win didn't seem to create a legend to anything like the same extent that the "Curse of the Bambino" did.

When you start talking about waits of over 85 years, you know there have been several fans that have waited their entire life to see their team become champions, and never got to witness it. Just think for a moment about how the world changed between 1918 and 2004 and you begin to understand the full extent of the wait.

Lesson to be learned from the breaking of this curse: you have control over your performance, past performances do not have to be an indicator of future performance. A group of players and coaches can change the identity of a club.

Chapter 7

Match Reports

Round 5 v Bradford (away) – 3rd March 2012

WHEN THE switch to the summer season came along, probably no club embraced the brave new world more so than Bradford. While a few other top clubs shunned the idea of an 'American-style' nickname and didn't see the need for mascots and cheerleaders, Bradford not only conformed to the new ideas but committed to them. Their mascots Bull Man and Bull Boy were a strong presence on match days, but they also made the most of the merchandising. As the Americans would say, they made the most of their 'brand'. Results on the pitch kept pace with their marketing success, winning the second Super League season at a canter, the last before the reintroduction of the play-offs.

For the next ten years or so they were always either winning Super League or coming close to winning it. They rarely dazzled with their skills, but their combination of power and consistency made them a formidable force. Over the last few years they have been sliding down the league ladder and are nowhere near the side they have been, and not even the most optimistic fan would class them as genuine title contenders this season. All that on-field and off-field success in the past makes their financial troubles this year all the more baffling. Maybe they simply couldn't afford that success in the long term.

In April 2009, with Warrington one place off the bottom of Super League despite a talented squad, I sent an open letter to the Wire players and coaching staff. The letter was published by the *Warrington Guardian*. I'd had enough of the spectacular underachievement, I talked to them about having a sense of duty to the fans and being fully committed to being the best they could be. Quite coincidently I'm sure, the next fixture was one that Wire won 58-22 at Bradford. That match was a turning point, now it was the turn of spectacular achievement, back-to-back Challenge Cups followed by a League Leader's Shield.

Warrington fans had gone to that fixture in 2009 hoping for a victory, and now they travel with expectation. Other wins so far this season have been about class and dazzling skills; this one was all about winning in the absence of those attributes. They couldn't get the Ferrari started, so had to make do with the Volvo, not pretty but got the job done. Even the most expansive teams in rugby league have always acknowledged that they have to earn the right to play that style, and on this occasion Warrington could never quite get to that stage. They could have lost interest and started sulking when it became clear that, for one reason or another, they weren't going to blow Bradford away with a series of long-range tries from fantastic handling moves. Instead they showed a great sense of duty to the fans and commitment to the pursuit of excellence.

Every cricketer would love for the ball to be coming out of the middle of the bat with great ease on every stroke, every golfer desperately wants to breeze through the course in 65 every round and every football team would greatly appreciate it if every time they played was full of accurate, slick and incisive passing moves. Sooner or later every person who has ever played sport realises that this won't be the case. One thing that separates great players and teams from good ones is that ability to reach the desired outcome without the desired process.

Once again praise must be given to the defensive effort, especially close to their own line. They are having to defend too much for their own liking at the moment, but it says a lot for the character of the team that they only conceded four tries in the last two matches, despite an awful lot of opposition play-the-balls within 20 metres of their line. It's without the ball that a team's sense of duty, commitment and spirit are tested the most and so far this team are passing all those tests with distinction.

I'm a big believer in focusing on the process and letting the result take care of itself, but this process has to include what a team should do when on any given day the process isn't perfect or anywhere close to it. You might plan a big garden party with a barbecue, but if it pours down with rain, you don't cancel the party, you just move it inside.

If they play like this every week they won't finish top this season, if every time they play like this they win, they will finish top this season.

Final score: Bradford 10 Wire 23

Round 6 v Leeds (away) 9th March 2012

LEEDS HAVE been the dominant force in the last few years of Super League, something they have managed to do without ever looking that dominant. Winning five of the last seven Grand Finals has without question made them the most successful team in that period. These successes have more been down to them winning when it matters than winning all the time. Not only do they know how to get to Old Trafford, they also know how to win when they get there. Outside of London, Leeds is comfortably the biggest of the populations of places in Super League, so perhaps their healthy average attendance of around 15,000 should be even better.

Until Don Revie came along to manage the football team in the 1960s, Leeds was most definitely a rugby league and cricket city, not a football city. The success that Revie brought to Leeds United created a monster of a club that, even now Leeds are not in the top flight, still attracts much bigger crowds than the rugby league champions. They have always been classed as one of the big rugby league clubs, but until this current generation of players they had been known as mass underachievers when it came to winning championships. The current team has a combination of the players who have been there and won several Grand Finals and along with some talented youngsters, it threatens to be a dangerous mix. Even if they don't finish particularly high up in the table, no one will count Leeds out of the running to be champions until they have been well and truly knocked out of the play-offs. Warrington know as well as anyone that it doesn't matter where Leeds finish in the table, they will be a threat in the play-offs.

The fact that a narrow defeat at the home of the world champions, with arguably their most important player, Michael Monaghan, missing, still feels like a devastating defeat, is a great sign of how the club have progressed from the dark days of melancholy-filled mediocrity. Other first-team regulars were missing, most notably Hodgson and Bridge, and Wire were unlucky with a few calls, but this is no time to be making excuses. Hopefully more will be learnt from games like this than from any number of 50-point wins at home to bottom-half teams.

There is no doubt that this Warrington team will make the play-offs, virtually no doubt that they will finish in the top four. A big part of the regular season has to be treating it as practice and opportunities to learn for the play-offs. Two aspects of this game were the two big tests Warrington must pass if they are going to have the best chance of triumphing at Old Trafford. One is learning to play better with a wet ball – it is a shame that a summer sport's biggest prize gets decided in a usually wet and drizzly autumn, but that is the way it is and Warrington have to deal with that. The other one is that they have to learn to beat top class teams in close games when it matters. On this occasion they failed both tests on the scoreboard. The fact that they kept the game so close despite way too many handling errors for their liking is once again a testament to their defence and their spirit. In this match the vast majority of the handling errors were not the sort I have written about before, those that come about from forcing a pass or an offload and it not paying off. Most of the errors this time were more basic handling errors, either in contact or from a straightforward pass.

Growing up watching Warrington I had often felt that there was a lazy streak in the side, particularly over the last 15 years. Over the last three years this has been gradually phased out, with just a handful of signs of it over the course of the last season. So far this season it looks to have been eradicated completely, instead there seems to be a concentration problem. It has probably always been there but previously disguised by the lazy streak. A sloppy pass when in good position to score, a loose carry when going into contact or maybe a silly and inexcusable penalty. In any sport the biggest prizes can be decided by split seconds of action, often the deciding factor being a lack of concentration at a vital moment. Of course all teams are looking to rid themselves of these errors. Warrington have worked so hard to get to the stage where there is very little else to improve upon.

I am still confident that this team will finish top of the league again this season, with lots of big wins, entertaining rugby league and better performances than we have seen so far, especially when the weather improves. The ultimate goal is of course to win the Grand Final and there are still maybe a few pieces of the jigsaw missing right now, but this hard-working group of players and coaches have plenty of time to find the pieces and I believe they will.

Final score: Leeds 26 Wire 18

Round 7 v Wakefield (home) – 18th March 2012

WAKEFIELD IS one of the smaller cities in the country, the sort where you constantly have to remind yourself it's a city rather than a town. Other than rugby league it's hard to think what the city is famous for. The rugby team were always distinctive because of their name, one of those clubs that had an unusual name that no Football League team had. When the summer switch came they embraced the new without ditching the old to become the Wakefield Trinity Wildcats. They have been described as the great survivors of the Super League era, often on the brink of getting relegated or not being granted a Super League licence, but they keep managing to keep their heads above water financially and put a team out on the park.

It's not only been a case of scratching around at the bottom of the table in Super League as they have made the play-offs. Although I would like to see this great game spread its boundaries, I wouldn't want it to be at the expense of traditional clubs like Wakefield. They have not always been merely survivors, they've had Challenge Cup successes and won two championships back in the 1960s.

If we are honest I think most of us were expecting to see around 60 points scored in this game, but what we weren't expecting was Wakefield to get almost half of them. Maybe the Wire players felt a strong maternal instinct from the Wakefield team. That would explain the several gifts they gave them on Mother's Day by way of several penalties and handling errors. It's a good job that teams don't earn points for crossing their opponents' 20-metre line, because from my viewpoint in the West Stand I was way too close to the action for most of the first half. I'm sure Phil Clarke's 'margin meter' would've had a big win for Wakefield at some stages in the game.

Had you watched only the action between the two 20-metre lines then you would have said that Wakefield were the better side on the day and thoroughly deserved to win. However Warrington's superiority in what could be described as the "scoring zone" was just enough to allow them to edge past a team who have only won one game this season. All the Wakey fans near me were in no doubt that this was by far their best performance of the season so far.

When defending in their own 20-metre line Warrington showed their typical desire to not let their opponents cross their line. Even though they conceded 30 points, it was a superior goal-line defence that was one of the biggest advantages Wire held over the Wildcats. The first four Wakefield tries had to be earned the hard way and came on the back of long build-ups in pressure. The fifth try came from a break outside the 20-metre line. Conversely, every time Warrington managed to venture beyond the Wakefield 20 they looked likely to score and often did. The reason for this discrepancy was two-fold, one being the aforementioned superiority in goal-line defence, but added to that was Warrington's greater creativity when close to the line, in particular from Briers.

New players continue to look like useful additions to the squad. Chris Hill impresses, especially with an attribute so important to a prop, that being the yards he gains after the initial hit is put on him. Brad Dwyer made a steady debut, looking like a genuine hooker when he jumped out of acting half-back, the sort of hooker I'm sure players like to run off.

Again the performance wasn't what we all want, not even particularly close to it. On the plus side it was by far the best of the games at Halliwell Jones so far this season, with Wakefield putting in a surprisingly good performance. It was good to see the Wire manage to close out a close game and win when far from their best. They may not have quite been at the races, but were still first past the post.

Final score: Wire 32 Wakefield 30

Round 8 v Wigan (away) 23rd March 2012

AS MUCH as it pains us to admit it, we have to grudgingly acknowledge that if someone was to ask us which is the biggest rugby league club in the country, our answer should be Wigan. In terms of trophies won and average attendance over the years it is hard to argue with their boast to be the biggest. It is said you know you're in Wigan when you are in a pie shop and you overhear an old woman talking about "nipping down the blind side". Their love of pies is often quoted and equally often mocked, but it's a stereotype I don't think they mind too much.

If you want to wind a Wigan fan up, you are better bringing up their penchant for leaving a game early. Some say this started in the late 1980s, at the start of their dominant period in the game, when they were often winning by such a big margin that they didn't need to bother watching the last ten minutes or so. In more recent times, the 'Wigan walk' is more likely to be seen with their team in a losing position with a few minutes left.

From the late 1980s, through to the mid-1990s, they enjoyed the most dominant spell in the history of the sport, including eight consecutive Challenge Cups and seven consecutive championships. At this time they were the only full-time professional club, a source of much irritation to fans of other clubs, it really didn't seem fair. It was a bit like Barcelona playing in the Scottish Premier Division. In the 17 seasons of Super League, where all the teams are full-time professional, they have only won two championships and two Challenge Cups, so Super League does definitely seem to have evened up the playing field in that regard. Right now Wigan are most definitely one of the top teams again, Challenge Cup winners last year and champions the year before that. They are without question one of Wire's biggest rivals for the title this year. As we learn from a song from the terraces, Wigan are famous, just not famous enough for the Pope to have heard of them.

It's almost as if they are giving the ball and penalties away on purpose to test out their defence. Once again their defence proved good enough to win the game in this thrilling encounter, the best and biggest game of the season so far. In the second half in particular it was like a training session of defence against attack for long periods. Even the one try Warrington did score in that half came while defending. The fact that a Wigan team, playing close to their best, could only manage one try in a half when they dominated possession so much, says all you need to know about the Wire defence on the night. Especially when that try should never have been allowed, Hock's obstruction so clear it appeared to have been taken straight out of an American football playbook.

It was a fiercely-fought encounter that lived up to the hype, a tough game where some players seemed to think that any tackle below the eyebrows was legal. Sport Relief organisers missed a trick because as well as the socks and the ball they would have got a lot more advertising space had they produced branded bandages for both teams to use. A couple of particularly vicious incidents might have left observers wondering whether a player called Lauaki could be related to a referee called Silverwood.

For the first time this season a match had that play-off feel to it, with all the intensity a truly big game brings. After the defeat at Leeds I suggested that one of the most important areas for improvement was for this team to find a way to win close games, rather than relying on domination and big scores to win games as they did so often last season. In the two games since they have won both by two points, last week against a spirited and enterprising Wakefield side, this time against a genuine title contender on their own patch.

Hodgson's goal kicking has to be noted as a vital part of the win, but as with any win there were several factors that went towards it. In the first half they continued their trend this year of being ruthlessly efficient at getting the ball from their opponents' 20-metre line to their try-line, even against a top defensive effort from Wigan. Both tries were expertly finished, the first by Atkins and the second by Monaghan. Warrington's defence may have been far from perfect, the number of breaks and half breaks Wigan made was testament to that, but every Wire player's desire to make sure a break didn't result in points has to be admired, even by all the Wire haters out there. They seemed to have found a way to always defend their line as if they were two points ahead in the last seconds of a Grand Final.

There were only glimpses of the Harlem Globetrotters-style handling that has been a feature of several other matches, but I still think that willingness to express themselves played a big part in winning this game. After

Wigan's dominance in the first 20 minutes or so in the second half, Warrington found themselves struggling to get possession in Wigan's half. At this stage any other team in the league would be desperately hoping for a penalty or a handling error from the opposition to help swing the momentum. Instead Warrington created their own momentum shift with an outrageously flamboyant handling move ten yards from their own line that created a long break for Matty Blythe to get well into Wigan's half.

Still dropping too much ball, still having to defend too much, still not building enough pressure, still taking risks, still entertaining, still defending phenomenally well, still playing with great spirit and pride, still winning and still looking like retaining their League Leader's Shield.

Final score: Wigan 20 Wire 22

Chapter 8

Broken Sporting Curses – Manchester United

G ROWING UP as a Manchester United fan in Warrington in the 1980s and early 1990s wasn't too much fun. At school fans of Liverpool and Everton would mock us about how long it had been since United had won the league. Even City fans would pipe up, because they had won it in 1968, one year after United's most recent triumph. For my first few years of watching football I never even considered United winning the league being a possibility. A successful season would be winning the FA Cup and beating Liverpool at least once at some point during the season.

Then in the 1991/92 season it all started to change. They had got off to good starts before, but they hadn't lasted long enough to make us believe that they could actually win it. Now though it was Easter and with the finishing line in sight they were still in front. Just when they needed a few more wins to clinch their first title in 25 years, they started losing, three defeats in a row handing the title to a grateful Leeds United. The last of those defeats being at Anfield against Liverpool meant that the tortuous pain was as bad as it possibly could be.

Around the time of United's collapse, the lead singer of Queen had passed away. The day after that defeat at Anfield I was in school and a lad told me the following joke: "What have Freddie Mercury and Man United got in common? Both will never sing We Are The Champions again." I didn't rise to the bait, just stored the joke away in my memory bank. The following year when United by complete contrast won their last seven games to finally end the wait for the title, I found that same lad as soon as I could in school on the Monday, reminded him of his joke and told him that they are singing it now.

If ever the phrase "final piece in the jigsaw" is to be used in sport, it would be difficult to find a much better example of it than United signing Eric Cantona from Leeds in 1992. His unique playing style and flair complemented the outstanding players around him, but maybe as much as anything it was his complete confidence that had the biggest impact on the team. That group of players, along with their legendary manager, were responsible for waking the sleeping giant and turning the club into a trophy-winning monster. The fact that Liverpool and Everton have now gone 22 and 25 years respectively without a title is a source of much smugness to any United fan, particularly ones around my generation. Especially as those curses don't show any sign of being broken any time soon.

Lesson to be learned from breaking this curse: you have to put yourself in a position to lose the big one, if you want to win it. Losing is part of the learning process.

Chapter 9

Match Reports

Round 9 v St Helens (home) 30th March 2012

ST HELENS are the team that have most taken advantage of Warrington's mediocrity in the Super League era. Their winning run over Warrington lasted so long that it was starting to look like Wire would never beat them. It didn't seem to matter how far in front Warrington got, or how long was left when they got in front, how well Warrington had played or how badly Saints had played, Saints would always find a way to win.

St Helens is a similar town to Warrington in many ways; not far apart geographically, similar-sized populations and no football team within striking distance of the Football League. When it comes to counting trophies that's where the similarities stop as Saints are behind only their bitter rivals Wigan when it comes to trophies won, but the tide has definitely been turning in Warrington's favour over the last three years. While Wire have picked up two Challenge Cups and a League Leader's Shield in that time, Saints haven't won a trophy since 2006. Also in matches between the two, Saints moving away from their old Knowsley Road ground seemed to break the hoodoo they had over Warrington as last season Wire won both league encounters.

While they appear to have been on the wane over the last few years, they still have a habit of being good enough at the right time of year to get to Old Trafford. This year they will be looking for their seventh consecutive Grand Final appearance. Lately though they haven't quite been good enough to win the big one, losing in the last five finals. St Helens are far from being the sort of club comfortable wearing the bridesmaid outfit, they will be desperate to catch and keep hold of the bouquet this time. Just like Leeds, they are still the sort of team you know are going to be in contention for the title, and can't be ruled out until they've been knocked out of the play-offs.

Last season the first wake-up call came in the Challenge Cup quarter-final. Wire hit the snooze button because they had their eyes on another prize only for the big wake-up call to come in the semi-final of the play-offs, when it was too late to do anything about it. At least this defeat has come more than early enough in the season for them to respond to it, and for it to have a positive, rather than negative, effect on their season overall. Two things have become clear from this game. One is that the team's performances haven't been as good as they would like, or need to be to become champions. Papering over the cracks with a great work ethic and desire to defend can only make up for other deficiencies for so long. The other thing is that it became blatantly clear that no team can keep winning without the ball.

It's supposed to be the bookmakers' job to give one team a start, but Warrington took it upon themselves to give the team who have made the last five Grand Finals a 22-point start. Caught colder than an Antarctic breeze, for a while it looked like any size of defeat was possible. Once again Warrington's spirit and defence helped keep them competitive but they have to find some way of having a greater share of the possession if they are going to start matching last season's performances.

The offloads are becoming the big area of debate around this Warrington team. Saints had clearly done their homework, their players swarming around the Wire player being tackled and all being alert to a possibility of an offload, resulting in a lot of the offloads ending up in the hands of a Saint. Nobody is appreciative of an entertaining style of play more than me, even if it means the odd game is lost when it shouldn't have been. But it is extremely difficult to be entertaining when you haven't got the ball. A lot of the offloads recently have come early in the tackle count, with three tacklers in attendance and the ball carrier about to be dumped on their back. While this is often seen as outrageous confidence, it could be seen as a lack of confidence, as if the player is saying the only way of them making any progress is by making this miracle offload happen. Often these offloads are happening when there are no Warrington players available to run onto and catch the offload, which gives the impression that the player offloading the ball is doing so for the sake of increasing the number of offloads during a game, rather than being part of a team plan.

For me what sets Warrington apart as more entertaining than any other team is not the offloads, but more their willingness to pass the ball around in areas of the field and times in the tackle count when no other team would. They are also prepared to attack from near their own line, early in the tackle count and have a desire and the ability to move the ball to both touchlines. One aspect they seemed to have lost a little from last year is how hard they run with the ball. Nothing is more entertaining than a couple of strong runs from forwards, getting their noses through the defensive line, resulting in quick play-the-balls that allow Monaghan to jump and scoot out of acting half-back and setting up one of those free-flowing handling moves to be unleashed on a back-pedalling defence.

In the opening 20 minutes or so of this game Saints backed up the sporting saying that the best teams do basic things exceptionally well, rather than exceptional things basically well. Even Jimi Hendrix would go through the chords and warm up before producing a performance, and if his basic chords weren't right then Foxy Lady or All Along the Watchtower wouldn't sound right at all.

As Leeds showed last year, being champions isn't about being the best every time, it's about being the best at the right time. The season consists of 27 rounds played before the play-offs begin and that should be 27 opportunities for learning. Hopefully there will be plenty learned from this defeat. At their best I'm convinced they are the best in the league, but so far this year they have been far from their best. With their spirit they always have a chance in any game, but if they hit their best at the right time I'm sure next year these articles will be written by *Spirit of '12*.

Final score: Wire 16 St Helens 28

Round 10 v Widnes (home) – 5th April 2012

WIDNES ARE Warrington's closest rivals, geographically. Unfortunately there is a chasm between the two clubs in most other ways at the moment. This is their first year back in Super League after being granted one of the licences in last year's announcement. They are another club with a proud history that have struggled in recent times, spending more time out of Super League than in it. At the moment the only thing their team is competing for is the battle to avoid finishing bottom of the table. Currently they are miles behind Warrington in terms of quality of squad.

So the ammunition their fans tend to use to fight us with is their much more recent title wins. Two championships in the late 1980s, just before Wigan became completely dominant, were added to by a World Club Challenge victory over Canberra. The fact that Wire have never been world champions is a fact a Widnes fan I know often reminds me of. That they beat a team of Aussies who were probably a combination of jet lagged, drunk and hung over isn't something that lessens his pride at all.

By putting down a plastic pitch, the first ever in Super League, they have certainly made sure their re-entry into the league isn't a quiet one. Their chairman who loves the idea of the artificial turf has been quoted as saying: "If this had been invented before grass, grass would never have been invented." You've got to love his enthusiasm. Playing football on artificial grass is bad enough, but a lot of eyebrows were raised when it was announced it would be used for a sport where you make a lot more contact with the ground than you do in football.

It is rumoured that the Widnes players have been told not to wear long sleeves or any sort of tights for home matches, because that would make it look like there was a problem with the surface. Undoubtedly the pitch will be a great source of other income for the club, as they can hire it out for use throughout the week and not have to worry about it ruining the pitch for match days. To counter that it is unlikely that the club will get the Challenge Cup semi-finals that they used to get to host, and it does remain to be seen whether rugby league and artificial grass can go together.

It's that time of year when Super League coaches try to manage their resources as best they can, without asking too many of their players to play two games in the space of a few days. The strength of depth of each squad is tested and in their first game of the Easter programme coach

Tony Smith did choose to rest a few of his established players. Presumably the decision was taken with Monday afternoon's tough prospect in the south of France in mind. Another benefit of that decision was to give some game time to some younger players and to give other established players a run out in positions other than their usual one.

Currie did a sound job filling in for Waterhouse in the second row position. Hill and Cooper continued their good form this season, giving plenty of strength in depth to the pack. But the two young players that are the most pleasing additions to the squad for me are O'Brien and Dwyer. The club has been producing a steady stream of youngsters into the first team for a little while now, but they have all been either hardworking forwards or wingers. Every team needs its fair share of 'piano carriers' as well as 'piano players', but it is still great to see two youngsters coming through the ranks that can play in the pivotal positions of hooker and half-back and do so with plenty of glimpses of class already and masses of potential.

The game itself was one of those that nobody expected Warrington to lose, even when they slipped to a 12-0 deficit early on. Yet once again their continually impressive goal-line defence was put to the test. With the score still at 12-0, they had to make several tackles within a few metres of their line. Another try or two at that time and even the Widnes players might have started to believe that a massive upset was on the cards.

Once Wire got their fair share of the ball, there was only going to be one winner. They seemed to be running that bit stronger with the ball than they had in previous weeks, making it easier for Higham and Dwyer to get the team going forward and make occasional darts from acting half-back.

The Super League season is a long, tough one and at some point the depth of every squad will almost certainly be tested by injuries and suspensions. That test can happen at any time of the season. You hope it doesn't come during the play-offs, but from this evidence even if Wire did have several players missing by the time it came to the play-offs, that wouldn't necessarily mean the end of their title chances.

One of the toughest tests on the Super League fixture list awaits on Monday afternoon, so a solid performance while several established players were having a rest was as good a way as any to get ready for the French test.

Final score: Wire 46 Widnes 12

Round 11 v Catalans (away) – 9th April 2012

CATALANS ARE the team that allow the organisers to call it a European Super League, as in the current Super League they are the only team outside of England. Based in the rugby league stronghold of Perpignan in the south of France, they are definitely a welcome addition to the Super League in my eyes, one of the all too rare good examples of how to develop a new franchise. Firstly the location was right, allowing them the chance to attract healthy crowds and making it easier to develop local players. When they first started out they used a lot of help from Australian players to make them competitive, but as the seasons have gone by they have fallen into line with the rest of the clubs in terms of the maximum number of foreign players in their team. Now they have created a team based around French power and aggression in the forwards, with some guile provided by some Aussies in key back positions.

Not surprisingly given the distance from the rest of the teams, they are probably the team that has the biggest difference between their home and away performances.

You always know Catalans away is going to be a tough game for anybody, but also any team playing them at home always thinks they might have a chance. Poor away form is another thing that they have gradually improved over the last few years. While I don't regard them as main title rivals in the way that I do Wigan, St Helens and Leeds, this year I would put Catalans in the role of the best of the rest.

Battered pride and bruised egos. A good time to take a few looks in the mirror. Last season Leeds had a humbling experience in the south of France and they used it as a motivation for Old Trafford glory. There's certainly no shame in losing to an exceptional side on their home patch, fellow title contenders who Wire might well meet at some point in the play-offs. The real disappointment came in the last 15 minutes when tries were being scored in such quick succession you felt like you were watching the highlights. Strangely enough until a fantastic solo try with 15 minutes to go, Wire were still in the game and had they shown more composure in taking chances then they might well have been able to snatch a dramatic comeback victory.

Overall there are still too many players not playing close enough to their best, but it certainly doesn't seem to be for the want of trying. Passes aren't hitting their targets, runs aren't being timed perfectly and too many balls are being lost in the tackle. I'm sure the practice is being done, and if there's ever a game where all the players do play close to their potential, then you would fear for the opponents. Even defensively they started to look a little ragged for virtually the first time this season. The line itself didn't look as organised and together as they would like. Plus I'm sure if they watch the game back the players would acknowledge that there was too much grabbing and not enough hitting. It's so easy to do especially if the attacking players are running good lines and using late footwork, but it is a classic sign that the defenders aren't quite in the right place and aren't using their feet as well as they would like.

Sport requires such a bizarre mindset at times. You are constantly searching for perfection, yet must acknowledge it will almost certainly never happen. What great players and teams tend to be able to do is accept those moments of imperfection and not let them distract them from their main goals. Manchester United had a far more embarrassing defeat than this in their season this year, but still look likely to end the season as champions. Like I've mentioned before the regular season is largely about preparing for the play-offs, especially so when playing against genuine title rivals. How much can you learn about yourself and your opponents, in case you have to play them further down the line when it matters most?

Despite the lopsided scoreline, in this case Warrington can learn from this game that they are more than capable of beating Catalans on their home ground. When it comes to the business end of the season though what a team is capable of is of no relevance, only what they actually do. Warrington need to build their belief that they have a greater control over the level of their performance than they have so far this season.

Even in a big defeat the game ended on a high with a fantastic try created and finished by Dwyer. Hopefully that will be a microcosm of the whole season, a few disappointments but finishing with one glorious triumph.

Final score: Catalans 44 Wire 16

BEFORE THE next Super League game there was the fourth round of the Challenge Cup. This is the round where Super League clubs enter the competition. Along with teams still left in the competition they make up 32 teams. Five wins is all it takes for a Super League team to win the Challenge Cup, but every team desperately wants to win the most prestigious knockout rugby league competition in the world, so winning it can never be described as easy. Teams are drawn out of a hat at random and the fourth round usually throws up one or two contests between a couple of big Super League clubs, but often this round means playing against a smaller club from a lower league and in rugby league terms a different world.

Warrington got such a draw this year, away to Keighley Cougars. They are only one division below Super League but there is a massive difference between the two. Playing in Super League means being a full-time professional, playing one division down generally means having another full-time job and getting paid a bit to play rugby league at the weekend. With this difference between the leagues and the type of game it is where it is so difficult for a team to use any sort of spoiling tactics, upsets in rugby league are extremely and increasingly rare. Yet sport being the way it is there is always a chance for both teams, and no matter how small that chance that is one of the aspects that makes the Challenge Cup so great.

For clubs like Keighley a home draw against a top Super League club can provide a much needed cash boost, as well as the honour of sharing a field with some superstars of the game. For Warrington it is a chance to give some young players a go in the first team, but Tony Smith still picked several established players too for this one. There was to be no fairytale for Keighley on this occasion with Wire running out 44-18 winners. The previous day Featherstone had showed that the magic of the Challenge Cup is still well and truly alive, producing one of those rare upsets with a win over Super League side Castleford.

Round 12 v Castleford (home) – 22nd April 2012

LIKE THEIR close neighbours and rivals Wakefield, Castleford is very much a rugbyleague place, but without the sport it's probable that very few people outside a 20-mile radius would have heard of the town. Yet they have been a near constant in the top flight in the entire history of the game. They've had some top-notch, trophy-winning sides over the years. When the summer switch came they were another club who committed to it wholeheartedly. It is perhaps a weakness of Super League that it has allowed the bigger clubs to be stronger consistently and made it more difficult for sides like Castleford to have the occasional brief spell when they can be right at the top of the game. Cas at the moment are the sort of club who could struggle at the bottom of the table, or reach the bottom end of the play-offs, depending on injuries they pick up and the form of key players.

There is no doubt who their key player is, the extravagantly creative half-back Rangi Chase, who is from New Zealand, but now somehow plays for England. He is a top-notch player, capable of the extraordinary, but I do have to wonder if Castleford would be better off without him and signing three or four established Super League players instead. While Chase is the most talented and skilful of their players it is his half-back partner, Danny Orr, who most embodies the spirit of the club with his impressively consistent, enthusiastic and professional performances.

After being destroyed by the Dragons and cruising past the Cougars it was back to the sort of game that the Wire have been best at this season, playing at home and dismantling a team from the lower end of the Super League table. The slickness of some of the handling and the tries that were scored were reminiscent of the big home wins early in the season against London and Hull

KR. In particular the ten minutes before half-time was breathtaking and brutal in equal measure.

Yet still we didn't quite get the 80-minute performance we are waiting for, and I'm sure the players and coaching staff are waiting for it even more. With it being 38-0 at half-time, with Castleford already starting to look dispirited, an 80-point haul looked a distinct possibility. Starting the second half camped within 30 metres of the Tigers' line only added to the likelihood of such a mass of points. But just when the Wire had their foot on their opponents' throat, they released the pressure with a few sloppy passes, handling errors and missed chances.

If it was a football team you would say they had slipped back into second gear and were prepared to cruise through the second half, saving some energy rather than pursuing a big score. But more so than in probably any other sport, it is far more energy sapping to defend in rugby league than it is to attack. So the players are more than aware that the best way of reserving energy is to keep running in try after try, as they had done in those dazzling ten minutes immediately before half-time. Instead it would appear that the precision of the passing, timing of the runs and catching of and keeping hold of the ball are still some way off where we all want it to be.

Having said all that there was still plenty to be pleased about in this performance like several slick handling moves that led to tries, the defence looking more solid than it had done in previous weeks and all this with a youthful team. Even without the front row leaders of Morley, Monaghan and Carvell, the pack was dominant, with the three 'Ws' of Wood, Westwood and Waterhouse being joined by the youthful energy and mobility of Hill, McCarthy, Cooper and Harrison as well as the creativity and versatility of Grix. Once again Dwyer and O'Brien showed they are more than just promising youngsters, of tries the Wire have scored from a scrum this season.

That ability to score tries from absolutely anywhere at any time, along with their brilliant goal-line defence, are the biggest reasons to believe that when the trophies are awarded this season Warrington will always have a chance, no matter how good their form at the time. Plus of course the factor of playing with the *Spirit of '55*.

Final score: Wire 32 Bradford 16

Chapter 10

Fleeting Triumphs and Near Misses

F OR THE record Warrington have been champions on three occasions, in 1948, 1954 and 1955. For one glorious spell they were one of the dominant teams in the land. All three championship-winning teams featured the great wing Brian Bevan, the man who has scored more rugby league tries than anybody else. Other club legends – second rower Harry Bath and scrum half Gerry Helme – featured in all three teams, but it is undoubtedly Bevan who had the biggest single impact on this glorious period. Maybe the lack of a championship since 1955 should be known as the "Curse of Bevan", but championship failures can be traced back to a time when Bevan was still in the team.

Having won back-to-back titles in 1954 and 1955, Warrington were hot favourites to win a third successive championship in 1956. They had finished top of the league and back in those days the play-offs were a much simpler affair – only the top four teams qualified for a straightforward knockout semi-final and final format. Finishing top of the table meant Wire would host the fourth-placed team in the semi-final. That team was

Hull and they weren't given much chance by anybody of stopping Wire from reaching their third consecutive final at Maine Road. Not only did Hull win, but they dominated to shut out Warrington 17-0. They couldn't have known it at the time but that was the first instance of Warrington seemingly being unable to win a title after 1955, no matter how good a side they had or how close they would get.

That shocking defeat to Hull signalled the start of a slump for Wire, the next four seasons seeing them finish no higher than seventh. In 1960/61, with Bevan still in the team, they put together a workmanlike side capable of grinding out results. Although the magic of the mid-1950s was missing they still managed to finish second and this time reach the championship final that was played against Leeds at Bradford's Odsal stadium. Playing Leeds in Bradford sounds suspiciously like giving up home advantage in a championship final to me, and Wire were outclassed by Leeds who won 25-10.

The rest of the 1960s saw Warrington embrace mediocrity. In the 1970s, Alex Murphy as player/coach inspired a revival that took them well away from mediocrity and 1973 saw them finish top of the table for the first time since 1956. But the play-off curse continued as they lost in the first round to eventual champions Dewsbury. The following year saw them win so many trophies that you got the impression if they entered the Grand National that year they would've won that too. Of course the trophy that was missing was the championship, it having been decided that the table-topping team would be crowned champions. Warrington's emergence as the kings of knockout rugby league that year didn't allow them to finally get their hands on the championship. An eighth-placed finish meant that even though they managed to win the play-offs, it was the Wembley triumph in the

Challenge Cup that was the biggest prize they scooped that year.

In 1986 they triumphed again in the play-offs over top-of-the-table Halifax in the final, but that victory did nothing to take the championship from Halifax. In the era of the team finishing top being crowned champions Wire did come agonisingly close to the ultimate prize on one occasion. Jonathan Davies proved to be one of the club's most inspired signings ever, from fierce rivals Widnes after they had encouraged him away from his international rugby union career with Wales.

In 1993/94 Davies had his best season in rugby league, providing the creative spark to make an excellent, hard-working and thoroughly well-organised side into genuine title contenders. This was during an era when to suggest Wigan were a dominant force would be a gross understatement. Back when Wigan were the only full-time professional club, not surprisingly they tended to win all the major prizes. It was a bit like watching a top-class heavyweight be allowed to box in the middleweight division. On this occasion though not only did Wire keep pace with them but so did Bradford. All three teams finished level on points, but Wigan had the better points difference and the championship trophy to go with it.

For us Wire fans who were around at the time the most distinctive memory of that season is the game against Wigan at our old Wilderspool ground. It turned out to be a classic top-of-the-table tussle with defences on top. Wigan were hanging on to a lead before Forster slid over in the corner to level the scores at 6-6 and send the 'Zoo' wild with celebrations. We should have known there would be a twist. Just before the hooter a soft penalty was given away, or completely made up depending on how biased the Wire fan you are talking to. Just as we were thinking that the subsequent attempt at goal would be

past, we just couldn't help but get carried away again. We had a team that was capable of finishing fourth and we had just added the best player in the world, playing in the crucial role of half-back. What set of fans wouldn't have got carried away?

There were two league games left to play when Johns made his debut. The first of those matches was played in front of a packed house and the club could have easily sold the stadium out twice over, such was the clamour to see the great man. Add to that the fact that we were playing reigning champions Leeds, and in rugby league world it was definitely the place to be that night.

Clearly even legends can be affected by nerves as Johns' hands were shaking so much he could hardly place the ball on the kicking tee for the opening kick-off. Eventually he managed it and from his towering kick Rob Burrow of Leeds was clattered by Wire's Aussie prop Chris Leikvoll and lost the ball. From the first play from the subsequent scrum Warrington scored a try in the corner through Henry Fa'Fili. Because of the occasion the atmosphere was already explosive, and that opening well and truly lit the fuse. The rest of the night was one of the best atmospheres ever at that stadium, possibly the best, as Wire went on to record a reasonably comfortable win against Leeds.

The following game was a trip to Hull FC, and by a strange quirk of fate it was already decided that Hull would be our opponents the following week in the first round of the play-offs. One thing was yet to be decided though, that being who would have home advantage for the play-off. Wire would need to win to claim the home comforts for their next encounter.

I decided to make a rare trip across the Pennines, such was the lure of seeing Johns play as much as possible for Warrington. My car had other ideas though, as on the

M62 with two fellow fans on board, the engine overheated and we had the ignominy of being on the hard shoulder with a smoking vehicle. To make it absolutely clear I don't mean smoking in any sort of good, young person's slang way. To add to the embarrassment not only did my car not get us to Hull, it didn't even get us past Birchwood or out of Warrington.

At least that meant we had time to be picked up by whichever roadside recovery agency I was aligned with at the time, and still get to a bar in town to watch the game. It turned out to be one that Warrington won fairly convincingly. Clearly Johns was the missing piece in the jigsaw, and what a piece. No curse would be powerful enough to overcome this man.

The Hull game the following week was supposed to be merely the first step in a hope-filled long run in the play-offs. Maybe we wouldn't quite win the whole thing, but we were definitely going to get close. Weren't we? No we weren't. Hull battered us from the start. Just before half-time with Hull 24-0 up I heard one of the most optimistic questions I have ever heard as a fan nearby wondered aloud: "What happens if it's a draw?" We just can't help dreaming.

The following season Wire were generally a little disappointing in the league campaign, just about being good enough to finish sixth to claim the last play-off spot, and that meant the first round of the play-offs was a knockout trip to Leeds, a team that had reach the last two Grand Finals. We travelled across the Pennines in the coaches that were paid for by the club owner Simon Moran, travelling with barely hope, let alone expectation.

We packed in to the terraced away end at Headingley, and slowly but surely the best Wire performance of the season was played out in front of us. Keeping it close was excellent enough in itself and at least that meant our long trip wouldn't be completely wasted. The longer the game went on the more we found ourselves daring to dream once again. With 99 seconds left Briers knocked over a trademark drop-goal to put us one point in front, a lead we just about managed to hang on to. It was the club's first play-off victory in the Super League era and one of the most dramatic wins in Wire history, with us unashamedly celebrating on the terraces.

On the coach trip on the way back we were pondering who our second round opponents would be, and for once this pondering didn't include any assuming we would win our game because we already had won it. Super League powerhouses at the time, Bradford were playing a competitive Salford team, and whoever won would host us in the next round. Plenty of people on the coach showed a blatant disregard for Bradford's recent history in the play-offs and were confident we would be making the shorter trip to Salford. Those people were proved wrong and we faced a very similar cross-Pennine trip, this time to Bradford's legendary Odsal stadium.

In a season when of all the established Super League powerhouses, only St Helens were having a good season by their standards, we easily fell into the trap of getting carried away once again. We only needed wins against Bradford and then Hull to book a place in the Grand Final. Bradford weren't as strong as they had been in previous years and although Hull had been good enough all season to finish second in the table, they didn't have too much play-off pedigree. Those two wins would see us face St Helens in the final, a team we hadn't beaten for over six years, but of course, anything can happen in a final can't it? They were the sort of thoughts going through most fans' heads as we went along the M62 in our convoy of coaches once again.

Wire kept it close again and when two tries in quick succession gave us the lead in the second half, we were jumping up and down on someone else's terraces in delirium, just like the previous week. By this stage there was no stopping our dreaming as in our heads not only had we already beaten Bradford, but defeating Hull was a mere matter of course. All that we weren't sure of was exactly how we would beat St Helens at Old Trafford. Would it be comfortable or by virtue of a dramatic last-minute score? Of course our dreams were rudely interrupted, not by St Helens, or even Hull, but by Bradford who showed all their class and experience to grind out a win and end our season.

Our next play-off campaign was over barely before it started, a humbling and embarrassing defeat in the first round in France against Catalans.

In 2009 we really couldn't care less about the play-offs, because completely surreally not only had we gone to Wembley, but we had won there. We had been waiting since 1974 for one of the two major trophies in the game and at that point we didn't mind at all which one came our way. Such was the poorness of Wire's start to that Challenge Cup-winning season that despite a strong second half of the campaign, they didn't even make the top eight to reach the play-offs. It is since this cup win and the one the following year that my desire to see Warrington finally be crowned champions has greatly increased. Until then I had spent all my life dreaming of seeing them win something and the cup had always been the more likely of the two. As the last few years have gone by the team have been running out of excuses and reasons not to win the Grand Final.

In 2010 they finished third, but they had comfortably retained their Challenge Cup, so now they were establishing themselves as the modern day cup kings;

experts in knockout rugby league, and that's what the play-offs are all about. By this stage I am starting to believe that if Warrington play their best then nobody can beat them. In 2010 two teams managed to beat them in the play-offs. Firstly St Helens gave them a lesson in how to play in the rain, then Huddersfield produced an upset win at the Halliwell Jones Stadium.

I managed to miss both games. First of all I was on a youth work residential in the Lake District, battling the phone signal to get text updates from home on the score at St Helens. The following weekend I was climbing Snowdon and then singing karaoke with some friends, again having the heartbreak lessened by only seeing the score via text rather than having every second played out before my eyes. I believe the crushing losses hurt a lot less when you don't see them for yourself.

That brings us up to 2011. After a crushing 47-0 defeat of Huddersfield in the first round, following on from topping the table, our hopes had never been higher. Then of course came that most crushing of losses to Leeds. I do have to add one more thing about the win against Huddersfield. After the match, Wire were presented the League Leader's Shield and several Huddersfield fans not only stayed behind to applaud the Warrington players, they also unfurled a giant banner in their own colours with the message "WELL DONE WIRE" written on it. Never had I been prouder to be a rugby league fan.

One of the reasons for the reintroduction of the play-offs was to keep more teams interested for longer and giving them something to play for, at least for the majority of the season. The flip-side of that is that those hopes of fans get built up so much more than they used to do, therefore they get crushed so much more often. When you had to finish top to become champions there were usually only about four teams in with a shout each season, and even the most deluded fan of another team would be hit by reality within the first ten games. Now every fan knows the fact that if their team make the top eight then at the most they only have to win four games in a row to be champions.

Winning four games in a row against four of the best teams in the league, even away from home, is so tantalisingly possible in the mind of any fan with the merest hint of dreamer in them. So as long as Warrington continue to have at least a decent side, every year will be looked upon as the one where they can finally end the long wait.

Chapter 11

Broken Sporting Curses – Europe in Ryder Cup Golf

THE RYDER Cup started in 1927 as a biennial match between golfers from America and those from Great Britain and Ireland. When the event you are trying to win is just one match played over three days every two years, the curse seems different. It's not the only thing the players are obsessed with as they have their own individual careers to worry about most of the time. Merely making the team can be a career goal, they can worry about winning it when the week of the competition itself comes around.

What also makes the Ryder Cup different from the rest of these curses is that they only had one opponent to beat. Losing over and over again at anything is demoralising, but when it's the same team handing out the beating then the demoralising effect is so much worse. Only having one team to beat also meant they had fewer excuses for not breaking the curse.

In the first 12 events Great Britain only won three times, including a big upset win in the last of those 12 in

1957. However this period was to look like the halcyon days of British golf, compared to the next 13 matches that consisted of one tie and 12 wins for America – a lot of those being by big margins. In 1979 the British team finally acknowledged that they could do with some help, and allowed players from anywhere in Europe to be eligible for their team. Top American players had been saying that unless their opposition became stronger, then there was no point playing the event.

The introduction of the continental players was the first step in reversing the fortunes, particularly as this included the inspirational Seve Ballesteros from Spain. He was the one European player at the time who didn't feel inferior to the Americans and had a true belief that he could beat them. The turnaround wasn't instant though. Defeat came in 1979 and was followed by a particularly severe hammering on home soil in 1981. After that came the next significant change, with Tony Jacklin being offered the role of team captain. Other than Seve he was the only European for the previous 30 years to have won a Major title, one of his two wins coming in America in the US Open. He had reached the top as a player and knew how to beat the Yanks at their own game.

Jacklin wanted the captaincy, but he made it clear he would only take it on some conditions. He did not want to be captain and to oversee more hammerings. His various demands could be best summed up by saying he wanted the European team to be more professional. Until this time the contest had looked like a bunch of enthusiastic amateurs taking on a team of elite professionals. One thing Jacklin insisted on was that the team travelled to America together and on Concorde for the 1983 match. The team outfits were of much better quality than they had been and players were made to feel special and as if they were on a par with the Americans. Along with this special treatment, the European players were left in no doubt that they weren't going over to America for a fun week away and to make up the numbers. Their new captain would be reminding them for months leading up to the match that they were going to America to win.

Europe travelled in 1983, looking to hand the Americans their first ever defeat on home soil. From the start the Americans could tell there was something different about this European team; they weren't just there to play, they were there to compete. For the first time since the tied match in 1969, it was truly a competition. The result was in doubt until the end of the final day's play. A magical wedge shot from Lanny Wadkins on the last hole helped America squeeze out a victory by the narrowest margin possible.

In the locker room afterwards the European players were devastated, they had given their all and stood toe to toe with the giants of the game for three days of competition, yet still they couldn't end the winless run. Seve looked around at his distraught team-mates and then gave an impassioned speech, asking them why they were so sad, when they had just produced a performance that had finally backed up the belief that captain Jacklin and Seve himself had been telling them they should have. The speech was perfectly timed and delivered, and the European players finally felt that they could compete with the Americans. Once you feel like you can compete with someone and deserve to be in the same contest as them, then it's not too much of a jump to believe you can beat them.

In 1985 with Jacklin still at the helm and Seve still in his pomp, the Europeans handed out a hammering of their own, and the Americans certainly weren't claiming it was too easy anymore. From that year onwards, the 13 matches have resulted in eight wins for Europe, just four for America and one tied match.

Lesson to be learned from breaking this curse: if you want your opponents to respect you, then you must first respect yourselves. To produce a championship perform-ance, you have to act like champions.

Chapter 12

Match Reports

Round 13 v Salford (home) – 6th May 2012

SALFORD ARE often the forgotten club when it comes to Super League. They are neither a new franchise in an untraditional area, nor an established powerhouse in a place full of rugby league history and tradition. They are sort of stuck in the middle of the famous rugby league areas on both sides of the Pennines. Of course the main problem they have is being located in such a strong football area, with both enormous Manchester clubs not far away. It's often mockingly suggested that Salford fans are just United fans who can't get in to Old Trafford for some reason. Given the size of the population they are surrounded by and how long-established the club is, their average attendances being around four thousand is at least as disappointing as the numbers at London and Huddersfield.

They have moved to a new stadium this year, with a capacity of 12,000, which is a bit like booking out Westminster Abbey for your wedding when you only have 100 guests. In the 1930s they were considered one of if not the best club in the land and they also enjoyed success in the mid-1970s, winning two championships. From the 1980s on Salford have been facing a battle to merely establish themselves in the top flight, rather than winning it. In the Super League era they have made the play-offs, but not at all often, and have never looked likely to reach the home of the other Red Devils. This year again they look to have the sort of team whose ultimate ambition would be to finish somewhere in the top eight, so they can say "at least we made the play-offs".

Going into a game without your first choice full-back, half-backs and hooker, you could expect a performance lacking in creativity, organisation and direction. For large chunks of this game, that is exactly what Wire produced. Ultimately it was only the excellent goal kicking of O'Brien that got the win. Against a decent Salford side who might just sneak into the top eight, but are highly unlikely to be a threat in the play-offs should they get there, a more comfortable home win would have been expected by most Wire fans. A look at the team sheet might have lessened those expectations somewhat as along with the pivotal position players of Hodgson, Briers, Myler and Monaghan, other established players like Westwood, Morley and Bridge were also missing. Just how many of those absentees were down to having one eye on the tough Challenge Cup quarter-final in France next weekend only Tony Smith can say for sure.

It was probably the first home game all season when I didn't feel I quite got full value for my £20. In the first half in particular the play was so conservative that it had the Wire faithful begging for the ball to be thrown around, even by those who have been critical of the team for overplaying earlier in the season. Anytime they did shift it wide they looked dangerous, especially when getting the ball to Atkins who created both Warrington's tries of the first half with excellent, orthodox centre play to allow Williams to score twice.

Overall performance will ultimately affect the scoreboard, but there is also no getting away from the fact that the scoreboard often affects performance. Salford's interception try came just at the right time for them to make the score 6-6 and keep their spirits up, giving them something to fight for, a spirit that might have been broken had the score gone to 12-0 or 18-0 early on. Also the closeness on the scoreboard seemed to inhibit the inexperienced Wolves team that was missing so many of its natural leaders.

The second half wasn't a great deal better, but there did seem to be an improvement in the urgency of the team to increase the tempo of their play. Most pleasingly there seemed to be a collective acceptance of responsibility to correct the lack of creativity and organisation from the first half, rather than waiting around for one or two players to do all of that for them. Another positive was that Currie looks to be the latest in the line of young players who is more than capable of establishing himself at Super League level for years.

A late flurry by Salford made for a jittery finish. Wire did manage to hold on for the win despite a collective brain explosion with 30 seconds left when they turned down the option of kicking for goal, something that would have run down the clock and finished the game – if I was a coach this would be one of the very few instances where my philosophy would permit my team to kick a penalty goal.

Overall it looked like one of those performances when a team tries to do just enough to win. In previous years Warrington have often slipped up with performances like this and done just enough to lose. Not a great game or performance by any means, but those two points might just end up being the difference between having home advantage in a play-off semi-final and not.

Final score: Wire 24 Salford 20

Challenge Cup quarter-final v Catalans (away) – 13th May 2012

WARRINGTON CLEARLY knew they had to be a lot better in certain aspects of their performance than they had been on the same pitch in the league game against Catalans a month or so earlier. That had ended in an embarrassing defeat but this one ended in a most impressive triumph. Warrington became the first team to beat the Dragons in France this year and the first team to ever beat them in that stadium in the Challenge Cup.

Catalans looked stunned and bemused by the way Warrington beat them – over-powering, out-enthusing and out-playing their pack down the middle. Rarely did the French team get up that head of steam that they thrive on, which results in quick play-the-balls and the opposition on the back foot which in turn allows that head of steam to become like an unstoppable runaway train. The speed of Warrington's defence line took that space off them, that space they so love to run into.

While still far from the performance the team is capable of and searching for, it was a performance that meant the gamble to rest so many players last week more than paid off. In particular a crazy spell at the start of the second half saw both teams playing with the ball as if it was a poisoned chalice. Also Warrington's penalty count was probably at least double what they would class as an acceptable amount.

Despite all those errors the team had a focus, determination and control about them that meant they never really looked like losing. When the draw was made I don't think I was alone in thinking that was as tough a draw as they could have got, so any win was going to be a good one. It's still far from out of the question that Wire might have to return to France in the play-offs and if so the memories of this performance and result will be of great benefit to them.

As ever Briers and Hodgson in particular always looked likely to create tries and Riley and Joel Monaghan always looked likely to finish them off. I'm sure all of them would quickly acknowledge that the real heroes and architects of this victory were in the pack. Even without Morley the club still have plenty of options in the prop position, all capable of defending soundly as well as giving the team great go forward, while Grix showed his fantastic versatility by offering yet another option at hooker in the continued absence of Michael Monaghan.

As they always seem to do the back-rowers Westwood, Waterhouse, Harrison and McCarthy brought impressive energy and work-rate to the team and led them in one particular aspect of the performance that although only considered a small part of the game might well have had a big influence on the scoreboard, that aspect being putting plenty of pressure on Catalans kicker Scott Dureau, who by the end of the game must have been dreading his turn to kick the ball.

Another game played this season, more lessons learned and confidences built. All three trophies still available to the Wire, still in position for a great season but so much more rugby league to be played.

Final score: Catalans 22 Wire 32

Round 14 v Wakefield (away) – 20th May 2012

WITH NO other pressing engagements on this Sunday I decided to make a little trip out for the day, rather than merely watching the game and heading home again. So I set off around mid-morning and headed towards Wakefield. Some people would be staggered that this was possible without a sat-nav – head east on the M62 and then follow signs for Wakefield, it really isn't that difficult. Never having been to Wakefield before I didn't know what was there to help me pass the time before the game and make the most out of my visit.

As I headed towards the city centre I spotted a couple of signs that were of interest to me. First of all I had a little trip around the Hepworth Museum, which displayed contemporary art. I have about as much knowledge of art as George W Bush does of world geography, but I do like to learn and try and stretch my mind. Walking around there while wearing a Wire replica top did attract a few funny looks. Perhaps rugby league and art museums aren't supposed to go hand in hand. From there I went to Wakefield Castle. There is not much of it left, but there is just enough to imagine what it looked like when it was all there. I also learned that is was the scene of a battle where Richard of York came to a sticky end in 1460 during the War of the Roses. Maybe I even stood on the spot where he died. At least his death helped people remember the colours of the rainbow – "Richard Of York Gave Battle In Vain". Another thing I could see from the castle was the stadium where Wire were due to perform later that afternoon.

Again by the power of road signs I found my way from the castle to the stadium, although I nearly went past it because it is not the biggest and it is set among some terraced houses. After walking around two sides of the stadium I eventually found a turnstile. Once inside I was faced with the wonderfully innocent and old fashioned prospect of being able to get to most parts of the ground. Always preferring to watch from the end I went behind the sticks, among fans of both teams.

Joyously the whole afternoon was one of those occasions that proved that segregating rugby league fans wasn't necessary, a bit like those Skins layers that the coaches wear as they take the players through their pre-match warm-ups. Throughout the match I was chatting to a Wakefield fan and among other things I remember him telling me about all the players that Wakefield had given their first taste of Super League, only for them to move on to bigger clubs and better sides. I nodded along in sympathy as I recalled a time when Wire fans used to say the same thing about some of their players.

It would be easy to criticise Wakefield's stadium but instead I will call it wonderfully old fashioned. At half-time I was getting the urge to do the old Wilderspool walk and swap ends. Had I done so I would have seen close up the five tries the Wire scored without reply in a dominant second half. Still without established first-choice players at half-back and hooker, this was a much improved performance from the previous round at home to Salford. The organisation and direction in particular were greatly improved and the creativity came in at appropriate times to produce the seven tries.

This was a performance that would have to be described as methodical rather than magical, but it was still impressive and entertaining. Clearly the game plan was to work Wakefield over down the middle and exploit the spaces out wide when they were there. From coaching teams myself I know that having a game plan is easy, but getting the whole team to stick to it is far more difficult. On this occasion the Wire team looked united in their belief that sticking to this particular plan was the best way to win the game. That this belief continued even when the scoreboard was level at the break must have been pleasing for the coaching staff.

The style of play from Wire on this occasion had more than a hint of a modern-day Australian style about it, sending lots of traffic down the middle of the field, being patient – not forcing tries to happen and being efficient at taking chances when within 20 yards of their opponents' line. The tries themselves did tend to come out wide, but only after the work had been done down the middle. Lots of them came from genuine moments of top-class quality, whether that was the precision of basic passes from the likes of Ratchford and O'Brien, more classic centre play from Atkins, the magical catch and pass tip on from Hodgson to create the first Wire try or the brilliant one-handed offload from Blythe on the inside to set up the game-breaking first try of the second half, scored by Ratchford.

Warrington did still offload the ball, but what was noticeable on this occasion was the quality of the offloads rather than the quantity. Players would have at least one hand free and a good hold on the ball and there was a player in support expecting to receive it. That was just one aspect of a thoroughly professional performance, one befitting of a team looking to be champions.

So far this season they have shown us different standards of performance and a few different styles of play. In terms of the style I think it could definitely be a good thing for the team to have several different ones that they are comfortable playing by the time the play-offs come around. For one thing that would mean they would have other plans to try if their first choice on the night isn't working. Another, probably greater advantage would be that it would be more difficult for the opposition to prepare to play against Warrington.

When Avram Grant, the Chelsea manager, heard the Manchester United team for the 2008 European Cup final, he said he had to prepare his team for six different ways the United team might line up, whereas for any other Premiership team he would only have to go through one or two possible scenarios. As soon as the match started he realised there was a seventh option and that was the one United had taken.

Knowing what your opponents are going to do doesn't always mean you can stop them, but not knowing makes stopping them even harder. Right now I would say Warrington are the hardest team in Super League to prepare for, and here's hoping as the season progresses they become even more unpredictable in that sense.

As for all those Manchester City fans who have ended their 44-year wait to see their team crowned champions, as I headed home on the winding roads through the Peak District I was thinking one thing – get in line!

Final score: **Wakefield 12 Wire 42**

Round 15 v Widnes (Magic Weekend) – 26th May 2012

TO THEIR credit the people in charge of running rugby league are always looking to try new things to help grow the sport. These ideas aren't always successful, but at least they are trying to make up for around a hundred years of virtually no spreading of the game away from its traditional boundaries. One idea they have had is to have one weekend every season where all the Super League teams play at the same venue. It started in Cardiff, then moved to Edinburgh, before going back to Cardiff for one year, and this year is to be the first that Manchester is the host city of the Magic Weekend.

Rather than the Grand Final venue of Old Trafford, the games will be played at the Etihad Stadium, home of Manchester City Football Club. With there being 14 clubs, there are four matches played on one of the days and three on the other. I think the dream vision was for all the matches to be played out in front of big crowds, with fans of each team stopping to watch every game. Unfortunately it appears the majority of fans just want to watch their own team play, so the total attendance for the weekend always ends up being considerably less than if the matches had been played at separate venues at the home of one of the two teams involved.

Originally the biggest part of the idea was to show the game off to a new audience, first in Cardiff and then in Edinburgh. Again this didn't seem to be much of a success with very few neutral fans making the trips to the games. Perhaps the one way the venture has been a success is the media attention the weekend attracts. The consecutive games makes for a great TV spectacle for Sky and even the BBC acknowledge the existence of the games a lot more than they do regular league encounters. It's also good that it's something different, that no other sport does, and that always attracts some positive attention.

As soon as I saw the big pitch, dry day and hot temperature I did start to wonder whether the scoreboard at a football ground would be able to go up to three figures. Right from the opening minutes this match never looked like being anything other than a massive win for the Wire. Playing against a poor team, on a big stage in perfect weather conditions was everything Warrington need to be at their devastating best, and for the majority of this match that's what they produced. For the fans it was a great day out at a brilliant stadium, in the Manchester sun, to witness their team destroy their most local of rivals.

There can't be many times through the history of rugby league that a team had a spell of around 30 minutes without scoring and still managed to rack up 68 points. So Wire are still searching for that elusive, complete 80-minute performance, but this was another display this season where the positives far outweighed the negatives. Wire were excellent going forward and had urgency in attack which helped produce some more fantastically skilful tries. The accuracy of the basic passing is now far improved from earlier in the season, an under-rated skill that gives the outside runners vital extra moments with the ball in the hand before the tacklers are on them.

Yet still in such a dominant and comfortable victory there was time for the defence to be impressive, particularly when close to their own line and especially so given that the game was won so early on. Even when 40 points ahead they showed a great desire to protect their line. The most noticeable case was late in the first half, when Atkins made a great chase back to prevent a Widnes try.

It was a great day out, fantastic atmosphere and a brilliant, devastating performance. The most pleasing thing overall for me was that the 17 players on duty included eight who have come through the club's youth system. For one thing this has given the squad a great depth, with each of them doing more than merely not letting anyone down when they come into the team. They add something to the performance and have all been deserving of first-team action.

If by some miracle all the squad is fit when the semi-finals and finals come around, Tony Smith is going to have a lot of players to choose from, but it will be that bittersweet moment for a coach when he knows he will have to leave players out who deserve a place in the team and will be good enough to play in a big match. That is far better than being the coach who has to choose a few players who fit into neither category. Another great thing about it is that it makes following your home-town team even more enjoyable when you can see the first team with several players in it who the club have developed through their youth system. Not all are from Warrington, but the club have certainly had a hand in the development of all of them.

It is safe to assume that Wire aren't going to win any trophies by beating Widnes any time soon, but it is still fantastic to go into an occasion like that with complete confidence in a big win and then see it played out as if there was no other possibility.

Final score: Wire 68 Widnes 4

Round 16 v Hull KR (away) – 3rd June 2012

DUE TO being at the Birchwood Carnival, helping to run a stall raising money for Warrington Youth Club, I didn't get to witness this match in any way, though I was able to listen to the last ten minutes or so on the radio as I was driving back in the minibus. It sounds like it wasn't too bad a one to miss. The disappointment is always less gut-wrenching when it isn't played out before your own eyes. Losing at Hull KR in itself is no great disgrace, but losing to anybody after having led by 16 points at half-time, let alone to a mid-table team, is a particularly bitter pill to swallow. From what I can gather it was another poor performance in wet conditions.

So rather than report on the match itself I will take this opportunity to write a summary of the season so far, a little half-term report. This stage of the rugby league season has the feel of the start of the second circuit in the Grand National. Any horse still on its feet and with a jockey on board has a chance to win, but some are in much better positions than others. To continue with that analogy I would say that London, Widnes, Castleford and Wakefield lost their jockeys a few fences ago. Salford and Bradford are still on their feet, but struggling to keep up with the breakaway pack. Leeds are hanging on to the back of that pack, not looking like potential winners, but from last year's race all the other contenders know that Leeds are capable of a devastating sprint finish.

Both Hull teams have established themselves among the leaders, but still have the look of teams that will once again find themselves wanting when the other horses produce a turn of speed over the last few furlongs. Saints could well be still a class thoroughbred, but at the moment are getting bumped around into making a few mistakes. If they can get a clear run in the end, they could still be in the final shake-up yet again. Huddersfield have looked top-class for the first couple of miles, but seem to have hit a wall at the moment, though it is still early enough in the race for them to catch a second wind at just the right time. Catalans are the foreign invaders trying to win a competition outside their own country, oozing with power and class, but not quite proven over the full distance yet. Wigan are looking every inch the complete thoroughbred and haven't shied away from hitting the front early on, showing signs of stretching the field out before it gets to the sprint for the line stage. They are travelling with great efficiency of movement at the moment and quicker than any of their rivals, but they still have lots of fences to clear and that wall can be hit at anytime, sometimes when you least want to.

That of course leaves Warrington. So far they have shown glimmers of being the champion horse that got into perfect position last year, before Leeds sprinted past them. But they have also not quite been at the races, making a few mistakes at some fences and not running as smoothly as they would like. However they are still tucked in nicely behind the leader, in perfect position to pounce on any slip-ups by Wigan and of all the runners the one most likely to beat Wigan in a one on one match race.

In 1955 the Wire lost five and drew two of their 36 league games, showing once again that champions don't have to be the best all the time, but they do have to be the best at the right time. As this team starts to make the long run for home, they won't want to make too many more mistakes at any fences. But despite not being at their best they look like they are going to be in great position when all the leaders make the sprint for the finish line.

Final score: Hull KR 23 Wire 22

Chapter 13

Broken Sporting Curses – Lancashire County Cricket Club

THEY SHARE the same tune of one of their favourite fan songs with Wire fans, instead of "oh Warry, Warry, Warry, Warry, Warry, Warry Warrington", it's "oh Lanky, Lanky, Lanky, Lanky, Lanky, Lanky Lancashire". Another thing they have shared is having to wait a ridiculously long time between title wins. In county cricket it is the County Championship that is the most prestigious trophy to win. Forget the hit and giggle of t20, or the slightly less manic one-day games, the County Championship is about a season of games that are set to last four days each. Four days of playing cricket for around six hours each day, and yet it can still so often end up in a draw. Some counties have big venues that are used for Test match venues by England, others have quaint little grounds a lot more akin to a village green feel. Playing in the County Championship includes a lot of travelling, a lot of staying in hotels and a lot of cricket.

Lancashire hadn't won the title outright since 1934 (in 1950 they shared it with Surrey), despite always being classed as one of the more powerful counties, with their famous Old Trafford ground being a frequent venue for Test matches. With cricket being the game it is, the weather can have a big say in the outcome of any match, and in turn the outcome of any County Championship season. So Lancashire had the peculiarity of a drought that was blamed on the rain. Stereotypical thoughts of Manchester rain were often given as a reason for Lancashire's long wait for a County Championship title. Too many rain-affected drawn matches would count against them come the end of the season, although I'm sure that if each year's squad were honest, there was always at least one other reason for not clinching the title.

Such is the complexity of the County Championship scoring system that it cannot always be too straightforward to work out exactly where a title campaign went wrong. Bonus points for first inning batting totals and first innings wickets taken can often lead to a somewhat farcical situation of the title being clinched by one player stroking a four through the covers halfway through the second morning of a match that they might well go on to lose. Give me a Grand Final to decide the champions any day.

One thing that Lancashire couldn't blame their winless years on was a lack of playing talent. As well as a host of England internationals over the years they have had some of the truly great international stars as their overseas player for the season. During the 1990s their overseas star was the cricketing genius Wasim Akram from Pakistan, one of the best bowlers of all time, a genuinely fast left-arm swing bowler who could get the ball to move all over the place. He was also a more than useful batsman capable of playing match-winning innings. In the 21st century they had the Sri Lankan spin master Muttiah Muralitharan, another of the game's greatest ever bowlers, a deadly accurate off-spinner capable of turning the ball enormous distances and even capable of spinning it the other way too. If you were to be trying to pick an all time World Cricket team, then you could make a strong case for both of these players to be in it. In the 1970s Lancashire could call upon the legendary West Indies skipper Clive Lloyd, a devastatingly brilliant batsman who was the captain that turned the West Indies into the dominant force they were in the late seventies and through the 1980s.

In 2011 Lancashire started the season with their smallest squad in living memory. The cost of the refurbishing of their Old Trafford ground meant that they couldn't afford to keep some players on. The building work meant that they wouldn't be able to play any County Championship games there, instead playing at much smaller grounds in Blackpool, Southport and mostly in Liverpool. The squad was largely made up of players who had come through their own youth system, along with a few old heads who had been around the county scene for years. Their coach was also experienced and well regarded in the county game. Despite a largely unsuccessful spell in charge of the England team, Peter Moores had already won the County Championship with Sussex in 2003.

Their overseas player for the year was Sri Lankan international Farveez Maharoof, a more than decent player, but nowhere near the class of Akram, Muralitharan or Lloyd. Expectations at the start of the season were very low, apart from the one place where expectations really matter – among the players and coaches. That the young players all knew each other so well helped create a great team spirit that the more experienced squad members were more than happy to be a part of. As the season went on they found themselves in close exciting games time after time and a lot more often than not they found a way to win these games, thanks in no small part to that great team spirit. With one game to go they were just a few points behind the leaders Warwickshire. While Warwickshire stuttered to a draw on the last week of the season, Lancashire eked out another win and one of the most unheralded squads they had put together since 1934 turned out to be the one that finally ended their wait for a County Championship title.

Lesson to be learned from the breaking of this curse: sport success will always be more dependent on the team as a whole rather than the quality of individuals. Having local players in your squad that are truly proud to represent that team is always going to help. Using things outside your control as excuses for your failure is not a recipe for success.

Chapter 14

Match Reports

Round 17 v Leeds (home) – 8th June 2012

THAT WAS what we had been looking for all season. Those first 30 minutes were just about all you could ask for from your rugby league team. Leading 30-0, no major mistakes, excellent decision-making and some fantastically creative tries and all against the admittedly out-of-sorts reigning champions. Even more pleasingly and perhaps in the long term most importantly it was the best performance by the Wire in the wet for a few years at least. They managed to find the perfect balance between keeping things simple, to keep hold of the ball and go forward, with just the right amount of attacking flair and Leeds looked like they weren't expecting or prepared to deal with it in such horrible conditions.

If any young players out there want to understand what is meant by supporting your own pass and showing great desire to get up with a player making a break, then they should watch Riley's second try when he put O'Brien through a gap, never stopped moving and busted a gut to get into position to finish of the score under the posts. The fact that O'Brien showed the required composure to slow down and fully commit the full-back made it just about the perfect try.

It looked like one of those performances where all the players were very much on the same hymn sheet, never more clearly demonstrated than by O'Brien's two tries from kicks by Briers. Every player seemed prepared to run strongly with the ball, often gaining more yards after that initial contact from the Leeds players. Higham had what I felt was his best game for a while, possibly ever for Warrington, taking the team forward well whenever he was on the field, either from quick, accurate passes or from penetrating darting runs from acting half-back. The overall quality of the play-the-balls was exceptional all night, not the most exciting skill, but one that has such a big influence on the attacking performance of the team. When the ball was shifted out wide it looked like every player knew it was happening and understood their own role in that move.

Leeds showed admirable spirit to keep the score relatively close, giving the impression that all is not lost for the chances of defending their title. When they got within 18 points, they must have been hoping that the demons from Wire's defeat at Hull KR the previous week would come back to haunt them. While their attacking exploits and pace of play had seemed to have deserted them a little, this was one lead that Warrington never looked like losing. By limiting the mistakes and playing a more traditional style of wet weather rugby, Wire kept the champions at more than arm's length all night.

Probably the best all-round performance of the season so far, and yet still several hints that there is more to come, a great sign that Warrington might be timing their run to be at their best when they most need to be, to perfection.

Final score: Wire 37 Leeds 18

Half-Term Report

With no Wire match to report on during this mini break in the Super League season I have decided to take a little pause for thought. Here's a game that all Wire fans can play. Imagine all the players are fit and available for selection and the Wire are playing in the Grand Final tomorrow. Write a list of all the players you would be happy to see representing your team in that game, not just the ones you would pick, but how many of them if they were selected would you be confident that they would perform well for the side.

I got up to 26 on my list, which is fantastic, far better than in years gone by when the list might have been around ten and I would have been scratching around for another seven that would have to do. Now comes the difficult part of the game, choosing 17! After much deliberation I managed to come up with a 17 I'm happy with in that I think it's an exceptional match day squad, but I'm not completely convinced it's the best possible one from that list of 26 names. If I were to do this every week until the end of the season I am sure the 17 would change a few times, but for what it's worth, here is my list. I can only imagine how much I would have deliberated over it if I had actually been in charge of team selection.

Hodgson
Joel Monaghan
Ratchford
Atkins
Riley
Briers
O'Brien
Morley
Michael Monaghan
Carvell
Westwood
Grix
Bridge

Higham
Solomona
Hill
Harrison

No doubt a few eyebrows are raised upon reading that, so I'll try to explain. Probably the most noticeable omission is Waterhouse and I wouldn't have a big problem with him being in the Grand Final team but to narrow it down to 17 I had to be harsh on some players. Whether it's because he doesn't quite fit in with the team's defensive system I'm not sure, but he does seem to have become a player that opposition teams have enjoyed some success by directing attacking plays at and around him. Also I don't think he has the versatility of players like Grix, Bridge, Ratchford and Harrison. I have been impressed enough by Ratchford's skill, speed and versatility so I wanted to get him in the side somewhere, and I do think that Bridge makes an excellent loose forward.

Paul Wood would rightly class himself as hard done by, but the squad is well blessed with front row options, and again when it comes to versatility players like Harrison and Solomona have edged him out for now. On the subject of Solomona, with no game time yet this season this is a gamble of a selection, but I just wanted to add that bit of magic to the bench. Myler might well force his way back into my squad with some good performances, but I just think O'Brien brings more creativity and passing accuracy to the team, as well as his kicking and goal kicking.

The younger players who have come close to establishing themselves over the last few years – Blythe, McCarthy and Cooper – can also consider themselves unlucky not to be in the squad and I would have no doubts about their ability to perform on the biggest stage. Other more recent additions to the squad – Currie, Dwyer and

Rhys Evans – would also not let the team down. In fact if we do make it to Old Trafford I have a feeling that Currie won't be too far away from a surprise selection.

A lot of Wire fans might be happy that I'm not in charge of picking the team, but it's certainly a fun game and it would be interesting to see just how many different final 17s fans would come up with.

A couple of general rugby league comments before I sign off. One is a suggested rule change. I really don't like the fact that a team that has a kick charged down and recovers the ball then gets another set of six tackles. This is not because Wire are the best in Super League for putting pressure on kickers. I think that the rule rewards sloppy play from the kicking team or punishes excellent defensive work from the other team, or both. I suggest that if that team recovers the ball then they have one more tackle, not six.

Also with regards to the Exiles match, I do admire the RFL's innovation and willingness to try new concepts, but I'm not sure I can get fully behind this one. It's never going to be a rivalry along the lines of State of Origin, because I can't ever see a day when young rugby league players from England will grow up dreaming of one day playing against a team made up of Aussies and Kiwis, most of whom aren't quite good enough to represent their own country. It especially loses credence when one player can play for the Exiles one year and for England the next. I know they've tried it before but personally I would prefer to see a Lancashire v Yorkshire or East v West series, our own version of State of Origin. I know it's close to impossibly difficult to imagine us ever having anything that quite matches the Queensland v New South Wales series, but I think if it's marketed right and the series is committed to then it can be a success. There is plenty of history behind the rivalry, and as young players they will grow up representing Lancashire or Yorkshire, so why not continue with it at a professional level.

The build-up montages and mini documentaries really set the scene for the State of Origin and then it is up to the players to deliver and they so often do. I think that if they were to start it off at some of the smaller but good Super League stadiums, and get full houses or close to it, get the Sky machine on board with the marketing and make sure the players fully commit to it then it could be a success both as a spectacle and as an international trial. For the first few years at least dare I say you could even encourage the players to 'bring back the biff' a little, to build up the rivalry and get people talking about it, even those that aren't big rugby league fans.

Another option I've thought of is a four-team tournament every year – Lancashire, Yorkshire, Wales and France. Semi-finals are played one weekend with the two English teams kept apart and the final and third/fourth place play-off played on another weekend. This would help with the development of France and Wales as we desperately need at least one of them to be strong for the sake of the international game. In the short term I think it will also help the English players by having a couple of competitive representative games each year. Hopefully over time the semi-finals could be Lancashire v Yorkshire, because we would know that the French or Welsh would make a competitive final, that way guaranteeing one Roses match a year. Whatever the RFL decide the fans do have to take some responsibility. We can't moan about the lack of national press coverage for what we call the greatest game and then not support our own events.

Round 18 v Hull (home) – 25th June 2012

IGNORING THE scoreboard can be one of the toughest things to do in sport, whether you're a player, coach or fan.

If you did manage to ignore the scoreboard for the first 15 minutes or so of this game then I think you would have to acknowledge a dominant display by Wire over a more than decent Hull team. Watching from the East Stand you hardly got to see any close-up action in the second half, Hull's only foray into the Wire 20-metre area in that half coming in the dying moments.

Although I am sure they will be disappointed with the way they conceded the three tries, the Warrington players and coaching staff should be delighted with the way they responded to them. It wasn't a case of a dramatic turnaround, brilliantly changing the game plan part way through or changes to the personnel having an immediate effect on proceedings. Instead it was a firm belief that what they had set out to do was more than good enough to win the game, if they stuck to it and trusted it for the full 80 minutes. Also having a strike player like Atkins bang on form was always going to keep Wire in the game. The long-awaited return of Michael Monaghan was roundly cheered, and he definitely did influence the game in a positive way. There were not too many signs of cobwebs as he starting jumping from acting half-back, bringing players on to the ball with accurate and easy to catch pop passes and directing players around the play-the-ball area.

Hull took advantage of extra tackles to score the first try and then an offload in the middle followed by swift handling created an overlap on the left which they exposed to race to a 10-0 lead. Warrington got the ultimate reward for one of their trademark charge-downs, Carvell's block resulting in Atkins' first of his hat-trick. Hull stretched the lead to ten points again, before Warrington's left side created two more tries and an even first half ended with the score tied at 18-18. Atkins' second was the result of some trademark Warrington offloads, which produced a classic reaction from a fan near me as he watched the offloads: "No, no, no...ooh yes!"

The second half dominance was asserted gradually. A combination of strong running and excellent footwork resulted in lots of good play-the-balls, and that combined with a limited amount of handling errors and penalties conceded produced the territorial advantage that eventually influenced the scoreboard. After what appeared to be around the seventh final warning to Hull, Manu was sent to the sin bin for interference at the play-the-ball. Hull had obviously decided that their best chance for success was to slow Warrington down and that risking the wrath of the referee was a risk worth taking.

The sin-binning came at a time when Warrington were looking to finally put a bit of daylight between themselves and Hull on the scoreboard, and indeed they took advantage of the extra player to do just that. Once Wire were two scores ahead there was only going to be one winner. In the end it was an impressive scoreline against a team who could still end up in the top four.

This was the latest match to back up what I was saying in last week's article about how impressive the Wire squad has become. Hodgson, Myler, Morley, Westwood, Grix and Solomona were among the absentees this time, but while watching a match I find myself noticing who is playing, rather than thinking about who isn't. One of the most controlled performances of the season so far adds to my confidence in Warrington building up to their best form at just the right time.

Final score: Wire 40 Hull 18

Round 19 v Salford (away) – 29th June 2012

THE DAY before this match there had been a sporting shock of seismic proportions that sent waves all around the planet. Rafael Nadal was beaten in the second round of Wimbledon by somebody ranked 100 in the world. On this night Warrington were on the wrong end of a shock that will reverberate up and down the M62. For one of the first times this year we really noticed who was missing. Clear evidence of it not mattering how much creativity, class and skill you have, if you don't have the ball and you don't defend your line well, it's virtually impossible to win rugby league matches. At times this year Wire haven't defended as well as they would like, and there have been plenty of games where they haven't had as much possession as they would like. This trip to Salford showed the spectacular consequences of doing both those in the same match.

It wouldn't be a good idea to wallow in the negativity of this performance, although I'm sure aspects of it will be looked at and rectified, but it could well be used as one of those matches that act as motivation for the rest of the year. Of all the sports to be on the wrong end of a hammering, rugby league is one of the worst as not only do you feel completely out-played, you feel bullied, physically dominated and for males it can severely damage the masculine side of their ego. With the cameras on them as they gathered behind their try-line after Salford's eighth and penultimate try of the night, the Wire players had shock and embarrassment etched across their faces in equal measure.

Any performance has two main sides to it, one with the ball and one without. On this occasion the most alarming deficiencies were without the ball. Far too many penalties were conceded, which, as it always will, had a big effect on the balance of possession and territory. More worrying were the defensive errors. Maybe it was a classic example of just how much of a team game rugby league is, as a lot of players were defending with people next to them that they weren't that used to. Whatever the reason there were a lot of poor decisions made, lots of signs of not trusting the bloke next to them and when they did get to the right place there were way too many tackles missed and fallen off to allow quick play-the-balls. At least one try was conceded largely due to the first marker not doing his one basic duty of chasing the ball.

When looking for the positives in this game I'm tempted to use Brian Noble's line of: "The kit looked clean." But even in this shallacking there were positive signs as at 44-6 down it would have been the easy option to go through the motions or virtually stop playing altogether. Instead the team showed great spirit and enterprise to conjure up three tries, seemingly either unaware or unperturbed by the fact that it was virtually impossible for them to score enough tries in the time that remained to win the game. The fact that this fighting spirit was driven in a large way by two youngsters, O'Brien and Dwyer, made it particularly pleasing.

Wigan losing at home to Bradford on the same night showed how upsets in Super League aren't that uncommon, but also meant that Wire had missed a great chance to close the gap at the top to one point. But it would be completely remiss to write a report on this match and not mention Salford. They put in an outstanding performance, at the moment they look like one of those classic teams just below the middle of the table who can produce top performances, but can't produce consistency.

Nothing truly worth achieving is ever going to be easy, no glorious destination will have an easy path to it and how you deal with failure determines whether you achieve success. If I had been in charge of the music played on the team coach on the way home, I think I would have put a Kelly Clarkson tune on: What Doesn't Kill You Makes You Stronger.

Final score: Salford 48 Wire 24

Round 20 v Catalans (home) 9th July 2012

CONTESTS WITH Catalans often have the physicality of a boxing match and this was the third 'bout' between the two teams this season. The first game was the equivalent of a devastating knockout in Catalans' favour, then Warrington produced their own knockout in the Challenge Cup quarter-final, and this contest would have to be classed as a brutally fought-out points win for the Wire. Unlike football, some of the best rugby league games can occur when the defences out-perform the attacker. Whether a connoisseur of the game with many years of watching experience or someone taking a look at the game for the first time, you would surely have been impressed by much of what you saw at the Halliwell Jones Stadium on Monday night.

It is said that 90 per cent of defence is about attitude and desire, and both teams showed that in abundance. There were times when Catalans made breaks, particularly in the second half, but to keep a highly motivated side with the quality of Catalans to just one try was a great reflection of the desperation the Wire players showed to protect their line.

Two stand-out examples of such desire would be Ratchford's last-ditch cover tackle that just caused the Catalans player's left boot to touch the touchline just before placing the ball down on the try-line, and Atkins racing across as an auxiliary full-back after a break had been made, allowing him to be in perfect position to catch a crossfield kick and snuff out another scoring opportunity for the French side. These are just two examples of many great moments of scrambling defence.

It was one of those games where neither side seemed to have a weak defender, someone the opposition could target and get success from playing towards. Performances like this really hammer home just how much you believe in your team-mates and how much you rely on each other for success.

Among all the fantastic defence there was the brilliant team try that was finished off by Atkins. It was a classic example of something good coming out of something going 'wrong' for the attacking team. This comes about because it often means something has also gone wrong for the defence, as the break in pattern requires them to change their own pattern and this can be so difficult if the attacking team play with speed.

To start with O'Brien was caught on the last tackle and his planned kick option was taken away from him by excellent pressure from Catalans defenders. Wire were almost forced into keeping the ball alive so in quick succession Morley, Westwood and Harrison all reverted back to the simple basics of rugby league attack – run at a gap until a defender commits to you, then pass to your nearest mate. This resulted in Atkins getting the ball in a little bit of space, but such was the quality of defence all night that Atkins must have felt he was in oceans of space by comparison to the rest of the match. From there a perfectly weighted kick and enthusiastic and speedy chase did the rest to finish off a brilliant try.

As preparations for a Challenge Cup semi-final go, physically it perhaps wasn't the best, a smashathon against one of the biggest and toughest sides in the league, but mentally I think it would have been the perfect preparation for them. Their belief in their ability to battle for success in a big match càn only have been increased by this performance.

Final score: Wire 15 Catalans 6

Challenge Cup semi-final v Huddersfield (at Salford) – 15th July 2012

WARRINGTON'S FIRST visit to Salford's new stadium

had been one to forget but this one was most definitely one to savour. After many years of waiting, we currently not only have a Warrington team that go into big matches as the favourites, but can handle that tag with the greatest of comfort. From the first minute Wire looked better than Huddersfield, not dazzlingly or devastatingly better, but just that little bit better in every way that matters. Like two Formula One cars in a grand prix, one only going a second faster than the other one each lap, but by the end of the race the gap between the two is a chasm.

A brilliant 40-20 kick by Danny Brough proved to be enough of a momentum changer to result in the first try of the game. Warrington could have reacted to that by getting jittery or at least by being drawn into a closely fought 'arm wrestle' where there would never be more than one score between the two teams. Instead this team responded with the class we are gradually becoming accustomed to. It took the video referee almost as long to award Wire's first try as it did for some people to get out of the car park after the match. From that moment on there definitely only looked like being one winner.

It is easy to be motivated to play the role of a plucky underdog on an occasion like this, by scrapping for all your worth and refusing to be bullied and blown away. Being good at playing the role of the strong favourite is not so straightforward. The confidence should be there, but never to be mistaken for complacency. You must give the impression to the other team that you strongly believe you are better than them, while also showing them that there is no way they are going to work harder than you, therefore taking away their main chance to beat you. No matter what happens in the game you must give off that air of confidence in your belief that the scoreboard will reflect your superiority in the end. On this occasion Warrington most definitely had the look of a confident side, but still one that knew they had to put in their usual maximum effort.

I thought Hodgson had an outstanding all-round game and wouldn't argue with his selection as man of the match, but I was also greatly impressed by Hill's performance, especially in his first stint, the first 30 minutes or so of the game. It's probably long been the case that when it comes to handing out individual awards the 'piano players' almost always edge ahead of the 'piano carriers', even when both have done their respective jobs equally well. I have never really understood the point of man of the match anyway, especially in such a great team sport as rugby league.

This semi-final was a great example of the strength in depth of the Warrington squad. It was more than harsh on O'Brien not to make the 17, but Ratchford has been equally impressive all year and he revelled in playing at half-back, which is probably the position he is happiest playing. Of all the teams in the league I'm sure Wire are best placed to still win silverware even if they get a few injuries at the wrong time.

Out-sung and completely out-numbered off the pitch and completely out-played on it, Huddersfield can have no complaints. It was great to see the spirit among the two sets of fans still being so good, bringing back memories of that awe-inspiring banner the Giants fans unfurled at the end of the first round play-off match at the Halliwell Jones last year.

After a horror show on their last visit to Salford I suggested a Kelly Clarkson song, so this time I'm going much more old school. How about a bit of Doris Day: Que Sera, Sera...

Final score: Wire 33 Huddersfield 6

Chapter 15

Life As A Wire Fan

UNTIL 2009 life as a Wire fan was a bit like having 34 bad Christmases in a row. Every year you were promised a great present and every year you would be left disappointed. Some years you never even expected the promise to be kept, most years though for one reason or other we allowed ourselves to get our hopes up that Santa would finally visit us. It was a strange mix of always expecting to be disappointed, but often being strangely optimistic.

Any time you found yourself in discussion with a fan of an opposing team you needed to be Perry Mason to present a good case for the defence of Wire. Not having won a major trophy since 1974, it was difficult to stand up in the face of bragging from Wigan, Saints and even Widnes fans all of which seemed to find their way into Warrington in everyday life. Usually I wouldn't even try to launch any defence, a tactic that was best summed up by a brief conversation I had during my first year at university. A few of the other students in my class were chatting about the upcoming Grand Final, wondering what combination of Bradford, Saints and Wigan would contest the Old Trafford showdown. One of them looked at me in my Wire replica top and said: "Your team won't be there will they pal?" I replied: "No. Perennial underachievers I'm afraid. In other words, sh**e."

With the town's football team being so far down the league ladder that you can't even find their results on Teletext, the only team in Warrington to support really was the rugby league team. Once when my sister and I got into a taxi in Carlisle when we were kids, getting a ride to the train station after staying with our grandparents for a few days over the summer holidays, the taxi driver asked us where we were heading to on the train. When we told him Warrington he replied: "Ah, rugby league country."

As I grew up watching them in the late 1980s and early 1990s, they forged a reputation for being a tough team to play against who defended strongly but lacked the creative flair and firepower to match the big clubs and win any trophies. My most distinct memory of this style of play was the 1990 Challenge Cup semi-final. Playing against a far from star-studded Oldham side meant that Wire had a great chance of a first trip to Wembley for 15 years. They got themselves into a 10-6 lead and then set about defending that lead. They tackled for all they were worth, it felt like they were tackling for about a week but they did manage to hang on for the win. At Wembley they faced Wigan in the middle of their glorious pomp and never looked like winning.

In 2002 in the days when relegation from the Super League was a simple matter of whichever team finished bottom went down, Wire found themselves in a desperate state, scrapping to preserve their proud record of never being out of the top flight. We couldn't believe that we were finding ourselves checking to see how Wakefield and Salford had got on every week, so we would know just how perilous our situation would be in relation to our relegation rivals. Suddenly that boring mediocrity of finishing around sixth and never looking like winning a trophy looked like halcyon days of joyous times on the terraces.

They finished the season strongly and managed to get themselves out of it with a game to spare. Winning that game at the old Wilderspool ground that clinched their Super League status for another season was one of the best atmospheres I can remember being in at a Warrington game. With the result no longer in doubt with a few minutes to go all the Wire fans were singing and bouncing up and down with joy and more than anything else, relief.

My one lasting image of that day came with a few minutes left and the result in the bag. The ball was bouncing around in our goal area and Burns was the nearest player to it. He had plenty of time to pick it up and run it back into the field of play. Instead he looked around with a cheeky grin on his face and launched the ball into the noisy, celebratory Fletcher Street end with his boot and raised his fist in celebration to us fans at that end.

As the 21st century moved on Warrington started to create the opposite reputation from the one they had when I was younger. They had managed to become known as an entertaining and attacking team that conceded too many points to finish too high up the table. It seemed no matter what style of play they used or reputation they created they couldn't win a trophy.

Among the lacklustre mediocrity, there have been some horrific defeats, scores of around 80-0 at St Helens and something like 84-12 at home to Bradford. That Bradford result was made even more difficult to take when stories started to circulate around the town that the players had a barbecue at one of their houses the night before the game and were up drinking until well past midnight.

Generally life as a Wire fan brought little more than misery and mocking, with the occasional false dawn thrown in. Of course there was the occasional victory against a top team, but ultimately that only left us wondering why we couldn't play that well more often. One thing about being a Wire fan, just like a fan of any team, was that if gave you a sense of belonging and togetherness. Once we got a knock on the door. It was someone telling us that I had left my car lights on. He had noticed the Warrington Wolves sticker on my car and said he felt he had to help a fellow Wire fan.

Chapter 16

The Letter

THE 2009 season looked like being the most disappointing of them all for me and other Wire fans. The squad was quite possibly the most talented the club had ever assembled, yet they had a shocking start to the campaign. Such was the standard of their performances that they managed something that is as rare as a Wire win over St Helens – they made me angry. It wasn't so much the poor performances and the bad results that angered me, more the way they were playing the game. They looked as if it was a chore to play and as if they weren't enjoying it at all, it appeared they didn't truly care about their performances.

Team spirit also seemed sadly lacking. One of the incidents that tipped me over the edge occurred in a game where teenager Chris Riley was playing. He'd had a good game, arguably the best Wire player in a losing performance. With a few minutes left he made a handling error and looked distraught. I looked on in dismay as not one Wire player went over to him to pat him on the back and tell him to keep his head up. Being the sort of person I am, I didn't shout at anyone, hit anybody or refuse to ever watch them again. Instead I wrote an open letter to the players and coaches and sent it to the *Warrington Guardian*.

The replies on the website suggested I had spoken not just for myself but several other fans and when I put it on the BBC 606 website it even drew many compliments from fans of other teams. The letter read as follows:

To who may be concerned,

I wish I could speak on behalf of all Warrington Wolves fans, alas the only opinion I can offer is my own, but I'm sure several of my sentiments will be shared by many other fans. There are two words I want to talk to the players about, duty and commitment. I desperately hope I am reminding you of things you already know.

As soon as people pay to watch you represent their team and their town, you have a duty to give of your best. Commitment is about much more than trying hard for 80 minutes every week.

Let's start with that sense of duty. After this season's home game with Catalans, I was walking out of the stadium when I heard a father talking to his young son. What he told him was something along the lines of: "That's what it's always like, we never win anything, ever, I'm glad you've learnt that at a young age." I hope that makes you feel as terrible as I felt upon hearing that. You should count yourself incredibly lucky to have such understanding and accepting fans. It seems that as long as you make the play-offs virtually every year and get the occasional play-off game win and cup run to the semi-finals, then the majority of Warrington fans will be happy. If you all were at St Helens or Wigan I'm certain the fans would be demanding trophies of you. When I think of Warrington fans in particular and sports fans in general, I am reminded of a quote from Grantland Rice, an old American sportswriter: "For when the One Great Scorer comes to write against your name, He marks – not that you won or lost – But how you played the game." Fans just want to see you being as passionate about their team as they are.

Believe it or not, for a lot of fans, coming to watch you play is the highlight of their week. Often it is the case that their season ticket is the one luxury item they allow themselves to splash out on. So the next time you play, remember you are playing not just for yourself, your team-mates and your coaches, but you are playing for the people who pay your wages, the people who allow you to play the game you love for a living.

Baseball legend Joe DiMaggio was quoted as saying: "There is always some kid who may be seeing me for the first or last time. I owe him my best." Michael Jordan has said that he played for the one person in the crowd who had never seen him play before, and that he wanted to make sure they saw something he or she would never forget. If two absolute legends can be that mindful of the fans then I'm sure you can. This club has not been champions since 1955 or won the Challenge Cup since 1974, the fans deserve a lot more. At least when you score a try always celebrate with them, not just with each other.

I suggest during your warm-up for the next game, you pick out one face in the crowd. It might be a child, might be a man or woman of any age, maybe they're in a wheelchair, it really doesn't matter which fan it is. Focus on their face for a few seconds and then for that match feel like you are performing for them, remembering all they are asking of you is maximum effort. Imagine how disappointed they will be to see one of their heroes playing with anything less than that effort. It might just help if you make it personal, rather than just a mass of faceless people in the stands. After a game a lot of fans, particularly kids, come down to the front of the stands, hoping to get a closer look at you. Would it kill you to walk over to them and chat for a few minutes, maybe sign a few autographs? I know you're exhausted after playing (or you should be), but I'm sure they won't mind you sipping on your energy drink in between words. Certainly if you're not in the squad for a particular game I can't see anything stopping you doing this.

Also I believe the club runs a lot of coaching sessions in schools, how many of you find out when they are and see if you're free to go along? I'm sure the kids would love to see you. Being a role model is not a choice, you do have a choice as to whether you are a good one or a bad one. The fact that you have been born with the required physical attributes to play professional rugby league, grown up in an area that allowed you to play the game, been spotted by a talent scout and managed to avoid career ending injuries, doesn't make you better than the fans, it makes you luckier than the fans.

On to commitment, like I said earlier, this is about so much more than the 80 minutes. It's about all day every day throughout your career. How many of you do any extra practice outside of training sessions? Handling skills? Kicking? Footwork? Balance? How many of you watch extra video footage to help develop your understanding of the game, or get more feedback on your own performances? At your level coaches should be there to offer you tactical advice, set up a game plan for the team, point out strengths and weaknesses of the opponents and spot any ways your technique can improve. They should not have to motivate you to play the greatest game at the top level.

If you're lucky your career will last 15 years, trust me you'll be even luckier if after you finish playing you find something you enjoy as much as playing. You must have all started out playing as a kid, dreaming of the day when you could play at the same level as your heroes. You are living out that dream, you're living out the dream of so many fans, act like it. Play with great enthusiasm, with a smile on your face and dedicate every single day to becoming a better rugby league player. If you must drink alcohol (although I can't imagine why you are looking for a greater high than playing professional sport), then can it not wait until the end of your short career, or in between seasons, or at least be severely reduced?

A quick few humble comments for the coaches now. Looking at the players it would appear they spend too long pumping themselves up in the gym and nowhere near enough, running, passing, catching and playing together to develop an understanding. Don't forget there is a duty on your team to entertain as well as win, think which players would the fans get excited about seeing in the line-up. I'm sure most fans would much prefer to see a team that makes a few mistakes because they play so positively, than a team that looks predictable and afraid to make mistakes. In this relegation-free era, there is one less excuse for a negative, grinding style of play.

That's my tirade over, if any of you can look yourself in the mirror and honestly say you are already doing all the things I've talked about, then you have my utmost respect. Here's hoping you all turn the season around, whilst remembering only you guys can make that happen.

Yours in eternal hope,

Spirit of '55.

* * * * *

IF NOTHING else the letter turned out to be beautifully timed as in the very next game Warrington went to Bradford and battered them live on Sky. They won ten of their next 12 games and if not for a late season stutter in the league with their eye on Wembley, they would have made the play-offs, having been right down at the bottom of the league after winning just three of their first ten matches. That was the season they won the Challenge Cup for the first time since 1974, by far my most joyous moment so far as a Wire fan.

Before getting to Wembley there were two matches in particular that signified the change Warrington were going through, from underachieving mediocrity to becoming a trophy-winning team. The first was in the quarter-final when they were away to an excellent Hull KR side. At the time Hull KR were having a fantastic season, even threatening to break in to the top four, and were particularly dangerous on their home patch. Shown live on BBC the game turned out to be a cup classic, the sort where the lead changed hands several times and every time you started thinking one team was going to win, something would happen to change your mind.

After going toe to toe with them Wire still found themselves ten points behind with only a few minutes left. Stunningly two tries in quick succession gave them a two-point lead, only for KR to kick a very late penalty to goal to send the tie into sudden-death extra time. Any score would be classed as a 'golden point' and that team would progress to the semi-finals. Several times during the match itself there were times when as a Warrington fan you felt that the team had done the classic Wire thing of putting in a brave performance, but ultimately find a way to lose. When they were taken to extra time with that last-minute kick, history told us that heartbreak was on the way. This was the first sign that this team was strong enough to fight against history. In the extra time period Warrington dominated territorially, forwards ran so strongly with the ball it was as if the previous 80 minutes had no effect on them. After a few attempts Briers finally landed the drop goal to send us to the semi-final.

The semi-final was played at Widnes against bitter rivals Wigan, the team that would always beat us in a big game. We watched on in joyous disbelief as for the last 20 minutes or so of the first half Wire tore them to shreds, try after try flowed in and they built up a 24-point lead. It should have been a case of cruising through the second half but this team showed they still had some of the old traits in their DNA. Three Wigan tries without reply left us hanging on to a six point lead, praying for the hooter as the players looked to have completely gone to pieces and that this was going to be one of the bitterest in the oh-so-long list of disappointments. Once again though when it mattered they showed a glimpse of the team they were turning into, another Briers drop goal stretched the lead to seven, so much more comfortable than six, and then Hicks scored a try in the corner to confirm our place at Wembley and start the wild celebrations.

The final itself had a strange sense of inevitability about it as a strong and composed performance meant they never looked like losing. Wire flew in the face of all tradition by starting a big final by throwing the ball out wide, clearly something Huddersfield weren't anticipating. Three tries in the early stages of the game gave Wire a lead they never looked like losing.

To sum up that crazy season I wrote my own version of the song Hello Muddah, Hello Fadduh by Alan Sherman. The original song is about an American boy writing home to his parents about how bad a time he was having at summer camp, only for the rain to stop falling when he gets to the last verse, which greatly lifts his mood.

Hello Mother, Hello Father
Letter from a Warrington rugby league fan

Hello mother, hello father,
This season is a complete palaver,
Ever since you emigrated,
I'm afraid the Wire have deteriorated.
I went all the way to London with a mate,
Only to see them lose 60 points to eight,
You're old enough to remember trophies,
All I've ever seen is show ponies.
Every year they tease us with potential,
Only for opponents' laughter to become torrential,
Fans watch on as players come and go,
The pride of winning – we'll never know.
The only chance we have of winning,
Is if the rest of the league take up binge drinking,
At least you're old enough to remember Brian Bevan,
By the time they win something I'll be in heaven.
We lose at home, oh Mum and Dad,
Away from home it's twice as bad,
You were right to leave for a foreign land,
This lot would lose to bags of sand.
The players don't seem to care,
That half the fans have pulled out their hair,
At times like this I'm in dismay,
That to watch them they make us pay.
Wait a minute, they've stop losing,
Tackling so hard, they're leaving bruising,
As well as the spirit, they're playing with a grin,
Challenge Cup run, golden point win.
Opponents' egos need reassembly,
Beating Wigan, off to Wembley,
Challenge Cup win, gee that's better,
Mother, Father, kindly disregard this letter.

Chapter 17

Sporting Curses Broken – Australia Win The 1983 America's Cup

W E OFTEN mock the Americans for calling their baseball championship match the World Series, even though it is only called such after the name of the newspaper that sponsored it. Their penchant for calling the winners of any of their sports competitions world champions can't match the arrogance inferred in the title of the America's Cup sailing competition, the apostrophe suggesting that the cup belongs to them.

It stretches back to 1851 when some upstart Americans came to Cowes and challenged the best British yacht to a race around the Isle of Wight. When the Americans finished 21 minutes ahead the Brits were dumbfounded and were determined to gain their revenge. From then on Brits and Canadians would challenge the Americans every time they thought they had a yacht that could beat them. By the time it got to the 1960s the British and Canadians hadn't managed a victory and allowed othersnations to challenge the Americans. It seemed they no longer cared who had the fastest yacht as long as it wasn't the Americans.

By 1983 there had been 25 challenges in total, with France, Italy, Australia and Sweden all having a go, none with any success, so the Americans' winning run stretched 132 years and it was difficult to argue with that apostrophe.

In 1983 the challenge came from Australia, who had a mysterious winged keel added to their boat. I have no idea what a winged keel does but it certain conditions it made the Australian boat go faster than the Americans. The challenge was raced out over a best of seven race series. Until this point the Americans had never lost more than two races, but now they were tied at three races all and going into a deciding race. This got the Americans in such a flap that they held secret meetings and tried to prove that the now famous winged keel was designed in part by a Dutch scientist and wasn't entirely the work of Australians, thus making it ineligible for the challenge. It seemed they really didn't care how they kept hold of their trophy and weren't at all too embarrassed to try anything to find a way to beat off the challengers out on the water. Despite their best efforts they would have to try and win it fair and square out on the ocean.

Order looked like being restored, with the Americans well in front and the widely acknowledged best sailor in the world, Dennis Conner, in charge of their yacht. But then on a downwind section of the race the Australians made up a miraculous distance to get in front at the final turn, with three miles upwind left to go. Then came the frenetic finish, the Americans determined to give every last effort to get back in front and retain the trophy that they regarded as theirs. With a sense of wanting to vanquish the underhand Americans, whose actions outside of the water had created a great sense of injustice, the Australians were even more determined to make history. Somehow the Australians kept ahead and won by 41 seconds.

While the Australian Prime Minister Bob Hawke marked the moment by granting his public a national holiday, the American representatives were far from gracious losers. Television cameras and photographers were banned from an extremely low-key trophy presentation, a trophy that had to be unbolted from its place in the stuffy New York Yachting Club before being taken to Australia.

Lesson to be learned from breaking this curse: champions are made when nobody is watching. Doing the best preparation possible gives you the best possible chance of success.

Chapter 18

Match Reports

Round 21 v Castleford (away) – 22nd July 2012

AT HALF-TIME I was already composing my report for this match. I was thinking this was another one of those matches that was a sign of how much the team has progressed over the last few years. This game had potential banana skin written all over it for a few reasons – coming after the Lord Mayor's Show of the Challenge Cup semi-final, being away from home against an enthusiastic Castleford side in decent form and going into the game with a few players missing, including the talismanic playmaker Briers. Even just a couple of years ago it would have been one of those games that we might have half expected them to lose. Instead this team produced a first half display of excellence at both ends of the pitch.

Castleford must have wondered how on earth they were quite as far as 30 points behind at the break. It would have been interesting to see what Phil Clarke's 'margin meter' would have made of the contest, with Castleford enjoying at least an even share of possession and territory. Slick, accurate passing, excellent lines of run and fantastic support play saw Wire produce five tries, all goaled by the ever reliable Hodgson – which always makes the score look even more emphatic. At the other end that familiar desperation in scrambling defence was in evidence once again.

When Solomona went over early in the second half it looked as if it would just be a matter of how much of a big score Warrington would run up. Castleford and to an extent Wire themselves had other ideas. Immense credit must go to Castleford for ignoring the scoreboard and keeping their enthusiasm, which along with the invention of Danny Orr and Rangi Chase, playing at his mercurial best, gave Warrington just about all they could handle for the rest of the game.

Only the players themselves can know if there was any element of 'putting the cue on the rack' and losing focus. Two things they will definitely want to improve on were the number of missed tackles and the amount of handling errors in their own half.

Overall it turned out to be a fairly even game, but rather than swapping scores throughout the game, they exchanged scoring streaks, Warrington opening with 34 points and Castleford replying with 26. Neither team was ever that dominant to justify those scoring streaks, but sometimes tries come with pressure and sometimes they don't.

So far this season Wire are playing with the appearance of a team that is desperate not to peak too soon, like a middle-distance runner sitting on the shoulder of the leaders, not wanting to hit the front too soon for fear of being caught before the line. Coach Tony Smith continues to make the most of the incredible strength in depth of the squad, by giving virtually every player rests at times. Hopefully this will result in a confident and relatively fresh squad come time for Wembley and the play-offs.

One added bonus of the Wembley appearance is that it gives the players that little bit more of a reason to be desperate to earn their place in the side, just when they thought they couldn't possibly be any more desperate to be a first choice. It wasn't so long ago that if Briers didn't play then we looked woefully short at half-back, but now the options in those positions include Myler, O'Brien, Ratchford, Bridge, Hodgson, Grix and Monaghan as well as Briers himself. Even more pleasing is that that sort of embarrassment of riches is the same for every position.

Only time will tell whether the team are timing their peak to perfection or they are not quite good enough to be champions this year. Right now I still believe they are going to be good enough on the big occasions.

Final score: Castleford 26 Wire 40

Round 22 v Bradford (home) – 29th July 2012

WATCHING WARRINGTON this season gives you a similar feeling to that a kid gets when his parents tell him they are going to leave him in the house on his own for a few hours – you don't know exactly what's going to happen, but you know you're going to have a lot of fun. This was another game that consisted of a long spell of brilliance, yet still the wait continues for a full 80-minute performance of the highest standard. Maybe they will save it for Wembley and Old Trafford.

When it got to 32-0, it looked like a case of wrong time, wrong place for poor old Bradford, as if they were going to be the team on the wrong end of an absolute hammering that Warrington have been threatening to hand out all season. Yet just before half-time the momentum turned and the Wire seemed to take their foot off the gas in an all too familiar fashion.

As was the case last week one must acknowledge the spirit shown by the opponents. The terrible state the club are in off the field was always likely to either make or break the team's spirit, and it is to the great credit of everyone involved that it has clearly been the former. At

32-0 down away to a Warrington side bang in form and producing exhibition stuff, it would have been easy to throw the towel in and take a rest for next week's game. Instead Bradford seemed completely undeterred by the score and played with an admirable amount of desire.

Second half lapses in defence for the second week running will be cause for some alarm, but this was a game where most definitely the positives outnumbered the negatives. At times in the first half Wire were playing close to their best, some of the handling was basketball-like in its brilliance. Not only did offloads come, but they were expected by the whole team who were on the front foot and ready to take advantage of the offload. The first try set the tone, with an offload in the middle of the pitch followed by two quick passes from Monaghan and Briers allowing Evans to produce some classic centre play to expose the two versus one situation and send Joel Monaghan scorching down the touchline, the Australian then producing a fantastic finish.

From that point the dominance was maintained by some excellent strong running and quick play-the-balls that allowed the team to gain excellent yardage. But it was the offloads and the handling that really caught the eye. At times it really did have an exhibition feel to it and there were several genuine breathtaking moments as myself and the people on the terraces around me gasped and then applauded and smiled in admiration.

Once again Smith shuffled his pack, the most notable trump cards missing this time being Atkins, Hodgson and Bridge. But once again it didn't stop the team racking up a big score and another win. The lack of a sustained performance is becoming increasingly frustrating, but it also has to be noted that this team have become exceptional at amassing a lot of points quickly whenever they are in the ascendancy in a game. Often in rugby league both teams have spells of territorial and possession dominance. It's how you affect the score during your dominant spell that determines the outcome of the game. I really don't think any team in the league would have been able to restrain Wire during the opening 30 minutes or so of this game.

Final score: Wire 50 Bradford 22

Round 23 v Saints (away) – 6th August 2012

MAYBE IT was a curse of Knowsley Road after all – two trips to play St Helens away since they left there and two wins for the Wire. This victory was about as impressive as Wire have produced all year. After winning at Wigan earlier in the year and the Challenge Cup success in France they now have wins at the home of the three other clubs in the top four. Add to that the very impressive home beating of Leeds and they have a confidence-boosting triumph over each of their main title rivals.

It would need a crazily biased St Helens fan to argue that Warrington didn't deserve to win this one. For long spells in the game Saints were not threatening the Wire line and they never had a sustained spell of pressure. Warrington well and truly won the arm wrestle and the territorial advantage that goes with it.

With only four league games and a Challenge Cup final to go it is getting close to the time of the season when Tony Smith needs to decide on his best 17. Ratchford again showed his versatility and how he deserves a place somewhere in the team with a solid display at right centre. Myler reminded everyone of his credentials with his best performance since coming back from injury. As is often the case it was a matter of doing the little things well that made Myler's performance good, his ability to catch and then pass quickly and accurately inside the Saints' 20-metre line creating many chances out wide.

Defensively the team were as sound as they have been for a while and equally encouragingly there was no second half drop-off in the performance. It was another of those assured displays where the team look as if they are expecting to win and expecting to perform well. Despite there being a few players that often play in different positions from one week to the next it looks like a team where each player is more than aware of their job. The forwards are always prepared to do the donkey work, the three-quarters are equally prepared to help them out with it from time to time. Half-backs and hookers orchestrate the attacks, with the look of every tackle being part of the plan and no play being completely wasted. The joker in the pack is Hodgson. Ever dependable in defence and on kick returns, he must be a nightmare to defend against, never knowing exactly when he will chime into the line and what he will do once he gets there.

Overall though still the most pleasing aspect to the team is the spirit and enthusiasm with which they play. It's all the little things that show that spirit; kick chases, putting pressure on opposing kickers, congratulating each other on tries, big hits and try saving tackles, leaving and entering the field of play together. All those things that were so evidently missing about three and a half years ago that I found myself writing an open letter to the players. They all add up to something that trophies can't be won without.

Late on in this game Briers put a decent kick into the corner near the Saints line, and to be brutally honest the chase was awful. The fact that the poor quality of the chase stood out like a sumo wrestler in a jockey club just goes to highlight how good the chases normally are and how rare an occurrence a lack of effort is from this team.

No matter which individuals are lucky enough to be in Smith's 17 when the biggest games come around, we know they will be physically capable of performing their role for the team at an extremely high standard. It is far more pleasing for me to know that whoever the 17 individuals are they will be working as one team, united by a common spirit.

Final score: Saints 12 Wire 22

Round 24 v Wigan (home) – 11th August 2012

IN OLYMPIC fortnight, when all the athletes are trying to peak for one glorious moment of a four-year cycle, Warrington seem to be timing their attempt to reach peak performance to perfection with two highly impressive wins in the space of five days, over the first and third-placed teams. Just like against St Helens on Monday night, this wasn't just a win on the scoreboard it was a dominant performance, leaving opposition in no doubt that (Wire were) the better team on the day.

Whether the timing of the announcement of all the contract renewals was a deliberate ploy or not, it was a great example of how united this squad are. Squad is the key word this season as so many players have had plenty of game time and all have looked up to the job. This has led to a freshness about the team for this time of year, it has also created a desperation for each individual to play their best every week in order to make them first choice for the biggest games.

Over the last couple of months or so, Wire have regained that tendency from last season of getting off to flying starts. A good start against Wigan is particularly useful because it has the added effect of throwing Wigan completely out of their comfort zone as they are so used to getting in front early and bullying their opposition from there. This match did have that look of a bully in the playground having someone stronger than them stand up to them, leaving the bully with no idea how to respond.

As with many times this season it was the defence that laid the foundations for the victory. Wigan's normal dominance going forward was virtually non-existent, and as any team would in the absence of that gained yardage and quick play-the-balls they found it nearly impossible to create the attacking plays they would have liked to.

It was one of those occasions where the scoreboard was a great reflection of the game itself – 30-10, and Warrington were three times better than Wigan, three times better in defence, three times better in attack, three times more in unison, three times more aggressive and always looked at least three times more likely to score.

Next week in London might well be another occasion for Tony Smith to rest some of his players and hope not to get caught out. The thing that must be most pleasing for him is that no players are giving him a reason not to pick them for Wembley and the play-offs to follow.

As always the forwards laid the foundation in both attack and defence and the backs revelled in the space that was created for them. Having two top-notch hookers in great form has really added to the team's performance, both of them experts in getting the pack going forward.

When the sport's biggest prizes are handed out after one-off occasions then you can never guarantee success. All you can do is do everything to get yourself in the best possible form and physical condition for those moments and from what we can see Wire are in great shape on both counts. Hopefully Tony Smith will feel like a Gold Cup jockey sat on a thoroughbred, coming to the penultimate fence, pulling level with the leader and feeling that his horse has plenty left in its legs for the sprint to the line soon enough.

Final score: Wire 30 Wigan 10

Chapter 19

Lies, Damned Lies and...

THE AMOUNT of statistics kept on sport continues to increase, some far more interesting and revealing than others. In terms of them being true performance indicators I'm left wondering if the correct statistics are being kept and analysed. *Moneyball* is a book by Michael Lewis that follows the Oakland As baseball team for a season. They have the second lowest wage bill in the league, but consistently win more games than virtually every other team during the season. Billy Beane is the general manager of the Oakland As, and because of his limited budget he has to look for value for money in every player he signs. The way he goes about doing that flies in the face of a lot of established baseball 'wisdom'.

He picks his players largely from their stats, but he puts the biggest emphasis on the sort of stats that other baseball insiders don't consider to be that important. The results of his team on the field strongly suggest that Beane is on to something. It started me thinking about all the stats that are kept on other sports and whether the emphasis is being put on the correct ones, and whether other stats should be kept.

Rugby league stats tend to be a strange mix of Australian, British and American jargon. As with most sports the terminology is often confusing to all but the keenest of followers and shows little regard for the English language. Look at the Super League website. Their statistic section covers the following areas: tries, try assists, appearances, goals, drop goals, metres, carries, tackles, offloads, attacking kicks, runs from dummy half, tackle busts, marker tackles, clean breaks, 40-20, kicks in general play, missed goals, missed tackles, errors, penalties, red cards and yellow cards.

Looking at those stats from the point of view of trying to determine the value of a player to a team, obviously some are far more useful than others. Ultimately it's points on the scoreboard that determine the outcome of games, but if statistics are going to be of any great use to coaches they need to be showing how those points are created. So even all the stats related to points scoring aren't really all that useful in themselves. A winger might well have scored 30 tries in a season, but maybe ten of them his mother could have scored and all 30 would have been scored by any other wing in the competition had they been given those passes in that position. Also it says nothing of how many tries the wing should have scored.

Try assists also don't give a full picture. A wing could turn several poor passes from his centre into tries, and again the stat tells us nothing of the number of times the player should have created a try, only for him to not execute the pass well enough or even pass at all. Goal kicking stats are good to keep so you can monitor if you've got the correct bloke kicking for your team, but as a tool to assess the value of a player, it is limited to say the least.

Carries, offloads and runs from dummy half are more about quantity than quality. What we really want to know is how good those carries, offloads and runs from dummy half were. What did they create? Were they the correct option to take?

The kicking stats only tell us how often somebody does something, not how well they do it, or again whether it was the correct option to take. A 40-20 is when the ball is kicked from inside your own 40-metre line, lands in the field of play then bounces out beyond your opponents' 20-metre line. This allows the kicking team the put-in at the subsequent scrum, almost certainly guaranteeing possession. Undoubtedly they are a fantastic way to gain momentum for your team, but even on these we could do with knowing the percentage success rate of these kicks, rather than the total of successes.

Clearly if a player is spending too much time off the pitch because they have been yellow- or red-carded, then that is something you would take into consideration when assessing that player's worth.

Any team would love to produce many tackle busts and clean breaks, but as a reflection of that player those stats can be misleading. Some tackles are easier to bust than others. Clean breaks can be a result of a magical piece of footwork from the ball carrier, but often the break is created by a fantastic pass or a great running line from an option runner who creates the space.

Metres gained is an American-sounding stat, except they would say yards, and in a game where territory is vitally important, it would be an asset to have a team who are all adept at gaining metres. Once again though this stat far from tells the full story, as some metres are far easier to gain than others. For example let's say Warrington play out a set as follows; the opposition produces a great kick and chase, leaving Hodgson virtually nowhere to go on his kick return, so he only gains five metres. Markers are ready and defence well set when Riley scoots the next play, so he doesn't get far. Now the defence are really pumped up and sensing the chance to trap Warrington deep in their own half. Morley takes a drive down the middle, taking four of the defence to take him down, but still doesn't make any more than eight metres. Carvell follows the lead of his skipper and produces the same sort of run with the same result, both of them producing a quick play-the-ball. On the fifth play Ratchford arrives with some speed and footwork, runs at those same four players that have just tackled Morley and Carvell, one of whom has been left on the floor, one with his back turned and the other two still back-pedalling by the time Ratchford gets the ball in his hands, all resulting in Ratchford gaining 15 metres. Has Ratchford really done his job better than Hodgson, Riley, Morley and Carvell did theirs?

The tackle count is probably the oldest of all the rugby league stats, along with tries scored and goals kicked. Yet hearing that a player has made 48 tackles in a game does beg the obvious question: "Did he have a good game, or was he just in the way a lot?" Coupling the tackle count with the number of tackles a player missed does give you a clearer picture, but it is still far from everything you would want to know. Some tackles are clearly harder to make than others. A full-back being left one on one with Sam Tomkins or Rangi Chase, in a big open space, can surely be forgiven for missing a tackle far easier than somebody missing a tackle down the middle when someone has run straight at them.

Errors is probably the vaguest stat of all. Do all errors carry the same value? Is knocking on at the play-the-ball as excusable as dropping a high bomb that's swirling around in the wind when there are three opponents challenging for the ball too? Is a loose carry on tackle two, ten metres from your own line, as excusable as flinging out a speculative pass that goes into touch on the last play of the game when you are two points behind?

I'll now move on to the stats that I think should be looked at in great detail in order to get a true assessment of a rugby league player, starting with one that was on that list – penalties. A lot of tries at the top level come about when there is a break in the 'arm wrestle', resulting in one team either having more than six tackles in a row, or getting to start their set of six close to their opponents' line. Certain things cause these breaks, and I believe they dictate what stats are truly important.

A common cause of more than six tackles in a row is a defensive penalty. So it would be useful to know how often your player is penalised. As with most stats this would need to be broken down into more detail to give a true picture of the player. For example you would like to know what all the penalties are for. If they are mostly for high tackles then you either have a technique or temperament issue to work on. Also you would like to know when in the tackle count these penalties are occurring and how excusable the offence is in the coaches' eyes. For example being caught offside on the second tackle for being a fraction quick out of the blocks might easily be forgiven merely as a sign of over-eagerness, whereas a pointless flop on tackle five is likely to get even the most mild-mannered coach fuming.

A team starting their set of six close to the opponents' line is often caused by a handling error. Most of these errors come when in collision or when trying to play the ball quickly. Alarmingly I believe this was the biggest difference between Australia and England in the last Four Nations tournament, England making too many of the sort of errors you wouldn't be happy about your Under-12 team making. Such is the potential effect on the momentum of a game of handling error, keeping a detailed stat on this will tell you a lot about a player's worth.

I think 'number of handling errors in contact per number of times taking the ball into contact' would be the simplest and most effective stat to keep. Any time a pass is dropped you have to look at both the passer and the attempted catcher, so that would be complicated and often a matter of opinion. Any ball carrier knows that whenever he takes that ball into contact, it's their responsibility to keep hold of that ball.

Trapping your opponents in goal, forcing them to drop out under their own posts, almost certainly gets you another set of six tackles in their half. Many tries are scored from these sets. So if any kicking stats should be kept, then I would say you would want to know the number of times a player's kick leads to a drop-out and his percentage success rate with those kicks.

Outside those momentum swing factors most people tend to agree that the biggest influencing factor on the outcome of a game of rugby league is the speed each team plays the ball. Therefore I would suggest a great stat to keep would be the average time it takes a player to play the ball. I know there are other factors that influence this, like the speed of the previous play and how many people are involved in tackling, but I still think it would be an extremely useful insight when trying to assess a player.

The reverse stat could also be kept. Every time a player is involved in a tackle, what is the average speed of the play-the-ball of the opponent? Our chap who made 48 tackles might well not have missed any, but if they got a quick play-the-ball off the back of 40 of those tackles has he really had that good a game?

When done well, there is no doubt that offloads can cause havoc for a defence. So maybe there should be a stat kept on what percentage of the time when a player is involved in a tackle that the opponent manages to make an offload.

So I wonder if you could put together a team of players who were all high up on the speed of the play-the-ball stats, were best at limiting offloads, made the fewest handling errors per collision, gave away the fewest penalties and had a couple of kickers adept at forcing dropouts, then would the scoreboard take care of itself?

It might well be the case that many if not all Super League clubs are already keeping these stats, but are just not making them public. I am a massive believer in sport being about far more than stats. There are some things no stats can measure like character, team spirit, belief, ability to perform under pressure and desire. But if you have the technology and the manpower available to keep stats, you may as well keep the ones that are truly relevant to the game.

I can put the anorak away now and get on with the rest of the book.

Chapter 20

Sporting Curses Broken – Spanish National Football Team

W HEN ENGLISH football fans would be-
moan their team's lack of success and great
underachievement, we used to be able to console
ourselves with Spain being even worse. Before 2008 the
only trophy they had to show for their efforts was the
1964 European Championship. That was only the second
playing of the event, it was held in Spain and it was yet to
be regarded as the major trophy that it is now, hardly an
overly impressive list of achievements.

From then their attempts to win a major trophy were
more a case of a Greek tragedy rather a Spanish drama. It
wasn't even a case of coming agonisingly close on several
occasions and not quite managing to win the big one –
they never even made a World Cup semi-final. This from
one of the most football-mad nations on the planet, the
nation that arguably has the two biggest clubs sides in the
world in Real Madrid and Barcelona.

Major tournaments would come and go, each time in the
previews the analysts had to acknowledge that Spain had

a talented squad, but as the years went by no matter how much talent they had they weren't considered as potential winners, such was the extent of their consecutive failures. Expectations were never higher than in 1982 when they hosted the World Cup, only for them to be beaten by the most famous goal in Northern Irish history and then fail to reach the semi-finals from a group with England and West Germany. Perhaps their other great nadir occurred in 1996 at Wembley. When you can't even beat England in a penalty shoot-out, you must start to think that you are destined to not win a major tournament.

Someone in charge of Spanish football took the decision to start again and put some long-term planning in place. They focused on junior teams and a consistent style of play, believing that winning at age group levels would generate the confidence required to win at senior level. It has to be said they had help from a Dutchman, Johan Cruyff, who set up a style of play at Barcelona that ran through the club from Under-8 upwards, and encouraged skilful players who could control the ball and keep possession. Whatever the reasons, those Spanish junior teams started winning those tournaments, the majority of the players were promoted to the senior team and in 2008 that winning experience they had gained paid off with a stylish win in the European Championship, where they were the best team throughout the tournament.

On to 2010 and the Spanish came to the World Cup with possibly even more talent and now that belief that comes with winning when it matters. No matter how big the European Championship gets, the World Cup will always be a much bigger and more prestigious tournament. With that prestige comes a greater pressure. They had managed to win the European Championship but still questions were asked as to whether Spain could finally hold it together and win their first World Cup.

In their opening game they dominated possession against Switzerland but managed to lose 1-0. Now all the doubters and critics were back, Spain were back to their usual style of freezing on the big occasion and Euro 2008 had just been a blip. Next they faced a tricky game against Honduras and an even tougher contest against an excellent Chilean team. Any more slip-ups and Spain would be eliminated at the group stage and would have headed home in embarrassment. It would have been easy for all the old demons to come back into their heads, all the failures of the past dragging down their performance levels. Instead they ground out two wins and won the group.

Once in the knockout stages they faced local rivals Portugal, impressive South Americans Paraguay, and the World Cup specialists Germany. Each were vanquished by Spain, their control of possession allowing them to produce three consecutive 1-0 wins. In the final they faced a Dutch team who seemed determined to sacrifice their footballing soul in search of their first World Cup triumph. Normally Holland are known for their own fluid passing game, but faced with an opponent who could pass and keep the ball better than them, Holland set about the final with a destructive style of play that was intent on stopping the Spanish from playing rather than imposing their own passing game.

For two hours it looked like the disappointing game plan would be a success to a large degree, as the scoreline had been kept blank. With a penalty shoot-out, the wholly unsatisfactory way of deciding a World Cup final, looming large, again it would have been easy for Spain to shrink into the negativity of years gone by, settle for penalties and probably lose. Instead they kept pressing with their patient passing style and one of their great players, Iniesta, scored a winning goal in the dying seconds.

In Euro 2012 they entered the tournament as favourites. Now all the question marks of their mentality had been answered, it was a matter of how long their reign would last. As the tournament went on the critics of their playing style grew, people claimed it was merely as way of keeping the ball and that it wasn't that entertaining. In the final they faced an Italian side that had been impressive on their route to the final, particularly in defence. Spain tore them to pieces with a gloriously stylish and dominant display that produced a 4-0 win.

Lesson learned from breaking this curse: in order to get where you really want to go, you might have to take the long way around. The longer the journey the more enjoyable the destination. If you want to fix something, it might be easier to go back to the beginning and start again.

Chapter 21

Match Reports

Round 25 v London (away) – 17th August 2012

ABOUT 10.20AM I drove past Bank Quay station and caught the reassuringly modest and down-to-earth sight of Chris Riley walking to the station with his rucksack on his back. No high-powered sports car of a Premiership footballer, just a local lad walking to catch the train with his team-mates. Whether they travelled down first-class or not, unfortunately the train journey would have been the highlight of the day for the players.

It was one of those games where the excuses were in place before kick-off. Several experienced, established first-teamers were missing, and a few others had an eye on a much bigger stadium in London. However everybody involved with the club will know that nothing at all excuses this performance against London.

One thing that seems to be missing from the team's repertoire over the last few successful seasons is the ability to come from behind to win. You could argue that over the last three years they have seldom been behind, but when you think of St Helens in their Super League pomp and Manchester United over the last 20 years or so, the overriding memories are those wins that they pulled out of the bag when all seemed lost. Those lasting reputations can only be built from several matches won in those circumstances, and more importantly the more it happens the more the players believe it can happen.

I said last week that Wigan struggle in games when the opposition refuse to allow them to be dominant early on. Hopefully opposition fans won't be able to say that of the Wire for too long. After two immensely impressive defensive displays against St Helens and Wigan, London breached Wire early on and far too easily. It has to be noted that London produced a fantastic performance, half-backs Gower and Dorn pulling the strings expertly all night and so many willing runners off them, with clever angles to go with their keenness.

It is also great to see their club beginning to produce so many local players, which for me is the main argument for keeping a Super League club in London, the long-term effect of getting the game played more and more exposure in the capital. And you have to take your hat off to the exceptional job Tony Rea has done as an interim coach. It's amazing what a bit of team spirit and pride in your performance can do.

Of all the games this season I think this is the toughest to draw out any positives from. I certainly don't think any of the players will claim to have had one of their best performances of the season. The defeat may well have cost the club the chance of winning all three trophies available to them, but fortunately it doesn't really lessen the chances of winning the big two. In fact maybe it was a perfectly timed kick up the backside. Just when everything seemed to be progressing serenely towards the business end of the season, it was a stark reminder that each game is a new opportunity to play like heroes or zeros and anything in between.

In any walk of life sometimes you're the pigeon, sometimes you're the statue. You're not finished when you lose, you're finished when you quit. After the last battering the team got, at Salford, I suggested a Kelly Clarkson song for on the way home. Maybe this time on the journey home, they should have listened to Journey's Don't Stop Believing.

Final score: London 62 Wire 18

Challenge Cup final v Leeds (Wembley) – 25th August 2012

HAVING MADE the trip down on the train, a journey organised by people from Wigan – maybe they booked well in advance from the mid-1990s – I got to Wembley in plenty of time, taking my seat when barely any others were occupied.

High up in the second tier I would get a great overall view of the game, although I would miss the sounds of the impact, the facial expressions of the players and the close-up view of the skills that I normally get from the West Stand at the Halliwell Jones Stadium.

Leeds kick off with Wire defending the end that I am at. Chris Hill has the thankless task of taking the first run of the match into a highly motivated and energised Leeds team. For virtually the first time all season Hill is driven backwards and he ends up spilling the ball but a potentially disastrous start is avoided by Ratchford swooping on the loose ball and running it away from the try-line.

The first five minutes see both teams settle into the game with neither gaining any particular advantage. An inside ball to Rob Burrow on the last tackle around 30 metres from the Wire line is read like a book by Ben Westwood, although most would guess Westwood doesn't read too many books. His resulting crunching hit on Burrow not only serves to give Warrington decent field position, it also gets the crowd excited and gives his whole team a boost.

In the following set Warrington produce the sort of offloads they are known for. Around the halfway line Ben Harrison takes advantage of being left one on one with Leuluai to get away an easy and controlled offload to the supporting Mickey Higham, who darts down the middle for a few yards before producing his own offload. Higham's pass doesn't have the control of Harrison's and the ball hits the floor, but it lands in plenty of space and by this stage the Leeds defence is broken and the whole Warrington team is moving forward in support. Hill latches on to the bouncing ball and continues to charge down the middle then produces a perfect one-handed offload to Myler, who along with Hodgson has been especially quick to support the break.

Now the Leeds defence is on full-on scramble mode, all being drawn to Myler, Hodgson is still in support but with so many defenders advancing upon them he's not in a position any better than the one Myler himself is in. Just when everybody else on the pitch is either getting giddy with excitement or panicking, Myler shows fantastic composure to spot Joel Monaghan in acres of space on the right wing. After the composure comes the technical excellence to execute the perfect chip kick that floats across the pitch, in front of Monaghan who can run on to it and catch it without breaking stride. By the time he takes an excellent catch Monaghan is over the line and sliding in for the first try of the game. One of the great Wembley tries lights up the 2012 Challenge Cup final.

For the next few minutes Wire threaten to get off to a flier and run away from Leeds on the scoreboard. They look by far the more creative of the two sides and make a few half breaks. At one point Hodgson is put through a gap by Briers around the halfway line and he has a free run deep into Leeds territory, but his subsequent pass to Westwood goes to ground and somewhat harshly is ruled to be a knock-on. This judgement by the officials takes on extra importance immediately as Ratchford produces a one-on-one ball steal and goes in under the posts, only to see it brought back because of Westwood's knock-on.

Leeds manage to stem the flow and, led by some excellent runs around the play-the-ball by Jamie Peacock, get a foothold in the match. Three Wire errors in quick succession from the 17-minute mark allow Leeds to build some pressure. Firstly Atkins offloads the ball into touch to surrender possession on his own 40-metre line. Then Carvell is caught offside while defending on the 30-metre line and moments later with Leeds getting ever closer to the line Carvell is penalised again, this time for stealing the ball in the tackle, one of those calls that could have easily gone either way.

Now Leeds are well and truly attacking the Wire line. An inside ball from Sinfield finds Kirke on a rampaging run, right in the middle of Higham and Hodgson, one of Leeds' biggest players running at full speed at two of Warrington's smallest players. For a brief moment the old maxim of "a good big one will always be at a good little one" rings true and Kirke tramples over them and finds his way over the line. A minor skirmish breaks out between a few players, but soon they are distracted by the biggest downpour I have ever seen. It went from no rain, to a storm of biblical proportions in the space of a couple of seconds. Had Noah been in the stands the rain would no doubt have got him twitching. High up in the stands we were never going to get wet and it was impossible not to laugh at the people down in the front rows as so many of them scuttled backwards in an attempt to get away from the monsoon.

If Leeds could have asked for one outside influence on the game they would probably have said rain as they are well known as an excellent wet weather team, and they have won four of the last five Grand Finals almost always on drizzly nights in October. The rain is so torrential that the ball instantly becomes the proverbial bar of soap. Passing and catching isn't affected all that much, it is in the tackle that the ball can become particularly difficult to hold on to.

Handling errors come thick and fast with Warrington producing the first two followed by one from Leeds, all in the space of two minutes. Even when Leeds produce their error it turns in their favour when after the tackle that caused the spilling of the ball, Paul Wood and Ablett have an exchange of views that results in Wood landing a right hook on the Leeds forward. Sinfield kicks a goal from the resulting penalty to put his side 8-6 in front, and Warrington are behind in a Challenge Cup final for the first time since 1990.

The rain eases off to a light drizzle and Warrington set about gaining some control in the match. It looks like great defence might provide a momentum swing for them when Monaghan and Ratchford produce a fantastic tackle and bundle the Leeds player into touch, but instead they are penalised for continuing to tackle after the referee's call of "held". That's always one of the harshest penalties in rugby league, even more so where there is a noisy crowd of over 70,000 to drown out the official's voice. That penalty results in Leeds getting excellent field position and ultimately turning over possession right on the Warrington line.

As Wire try to run the ball away from their line they get one of the most common penalties in the game, that being the defence caught offside in their over-eagerness to keep their opposition trapped as close to their line as possible. That allows Wire to escape up towards the halfway line and the following penalty for a high tackle on Michael Monaghan as he went on a jinking run puts them in position to attack the Leeds line with 29 minutes played.

From right in front of the posts and less than ten metres away, Warrington have the perfect opportunity to attack in either direction. They choose to go left, slick, accurate passes from Monaghan and Myler leading to Waterhouse crashing between Watkins and Jones-Bishop and sliding over the line for the try. Hodgson's conversion puts Warrington in front 12-8.

The game settles down again and Wire's four-point lead looks like staying intact at half-time, until with three minutes or so to go Atkins loses the ball on the halfway line. Leeds take advantage of the excellent field position, get to the last tackle and put up a threatening crossfield high kick that would have landed very close to the Warrington line had Joel Monaghan not caught it and then set off up the field. Just when we are all getting excited as Monaghan breaks up the field into open space, we notice the touch judge has come on and is chatting away to Lee Briers. The judgement was that Briers had blocked off Hall in his attempt to get to the ball. Surprisingly with two minutes left of the half and being four points behind Sinfield opts to go for goal and cuts the half-time deficit to 12-10.

At half-time I'm confident that Wire are looking the better side, but not as confident that they will be victorious. I have a feeling that it just might turn into one of those games where frustration gets the better of the 'better' team and they end up losing. From our end it feels like we have been on the wrong end of some tough calls by the officials and even the weather has been against us. By the time the second half starts I have convinced myself that the Warrington players won't feel sorry for themselves and will be focusing on them being the better team.

The second half is barely two minutes old when the incident that was the most talked about after the game occurs. Hodgson runs the ball back from a Leeds kick and runs straight into a bone-shuddering hit from Leuluai. He probably extends his own record of being the most knocked-out player in rugby league history and also spills the ball. Delaney gathers it and runs in untouched to slide over. Not surprisingly the square goes in the air and the video referee has some work to do. Looking on the big screen at the opposite end of the ground it appears for all the world like not only a high tackle but a dangerous attack to the head with the shoulder. We can't believe how many times the official needs to see the replay, but as soon as I watch it back at home on television I can completely understand the deliberation. After several close-up views it's difficult to say whether the shoulder actually makes contact with the face or whether Hodgson's head is snapped back purely from the impact on the chest.

After about a dozen replays I'm none the wiser, so I'll have to defer to Hodgson himself who after the game told the television interviewer that there was nothing wrong with the tackle and "he just got me". While at Wembley the more replays were shown the more we worried that somehow the try was going to be given. So when "no try" was flashed up on the screen relief was the first emotion, quickly followed by confusion when "scrum defence" was also on the screen, meaning Leeds would get the ball from the scrum. Now we could deduce that it had been judged not to be a high tackle and that Hodgson had knocked on and either Leuluai had knocked on after that or Delaney was offside. However the decision had been arrived at, at the time it felt like another one had gone against us and I feared the players would be caught feeling sorry for themselves for a moment or two, just enough time to let Leeds score as they were starting possession around 20 metres from the Wire line.

These fears were eased completely when on the last tackle of that set great scrambling defence bundled Leeds into touch and several players raced over for encouraging back slaps. It was still possible for Warrington to lose this game, but it was clear they weren't going to lose it because they were feeling sorry for themselves.

An excellent set from Warrington leaves Leeds backed up to their own line and trying to run it out from there. Every game has momentum changes, some bigger than others and after 46 minutes this game had one – an outstanding piece of defence by Myler, as he flew out of the line and put a really big hit on Hardaker and drove him back behind the try-line to force a drop-out. Next came another controversial decision by the officials, one of those rare cases when they are technically correct but they still get heaps of criticism. When trying to field the drop-out, Briers fumbles the ball and slips at the same time. It looks for all the world like a knock-on and at least 95 times out of 100 it would have been given as one. But the ball just about went backwards out of his hands, until it hit the floor, then bounced forward.

A controlled set followed ending with a Briers chip kick for Joel Monaghan to contest with Hall, resulting in Hall being trapped in goal and another drop-out being forced. Leeds show signs of creaking and Wire shift the ball left to expose a lack of numbers on Leeds' right. Excellent, simple passes from Michael Monaghan, Hodgson and Atkins leave Riley with the simplest task of a clear five-yard run to the line before sliding over in the corner. One player who didn't even touch the ball probably had as big an influence on the try as any other player. Waterhouse's run was perfectly timed and angled to cause more than enough confusion and wrong decisions in the Leeds defence to create the space for Riley. A rare miss from Hodgson leaves the score at 14-8.

Just after Riley's try he, along with Myler and Water-house, slides Watkins into touch on the Leeds 45 metre line. From that excellent starting point to a set, Briers ultimately forces another drop-out with a well weighted grubber kick. Then comes nearly a carbon copy of Riley's try, this time it's Monaghan to Myler to Hodgson and then it's Atkins who has the joyous task of sliding over in the corner. Once again Waterhouse is of great use by not being used. Hodgson has his radar back on track and lands the goal to take the score to 20-8.

Barely five minutes later excellent last tackle defence causes panic in the Leeds attack with them around the halfway line. Sinfield feels the rush of defenders wanting to charge down his kick, so flings out a wild pass that goes behind all his team-mates. Keinhorst does well to conjure up any sort of decent kick, but it still results in Wire having possession on the halfway line. As if they were fed up with all the glory the left side of attack were getting, Ratchford and the Monaghan brothers produce a fantastic piece of blindside play with an interchange of short passes creating a break that nearly sees Joel score. Instead his resultant quick play-the-ball allows his brother to pass on to the charging Ben Westwood who looks hell bent on reaching the try-line. It takes four Leeds players to stop him, but somehow they can't prevent him from offloading the ball to McCarthy who has all his birthdays and Christmases come at once as all he has to do is catch the ball and plonk it down over the line to score in a Challenge Cup final.

A few minutes later Briers stroked over a drop goal on the third tackle to take the score to 29-10, meaning Leeds would have to score at least four times in the last 18 minutes to win and that was not going to happen. So that was it, that was the trademark burst of this Warrington team, 17 points in around 12 minutes. When they are good they are excellent at making the most of it.

Having looked like their plan was to grind Warrington down and pinch a win in a low-scoring match by kicking penalty goals, Leeds were forced into a more expansive game and it was only then that they looked like creating breaks. They even managed a couple of tries, but they were never going to be more than consolation scores. In between their tries it was Hodgson's turn to take advantage of the space created by Waterhouse's running off the ball. Hodgson took a couple of Leeds defenders with him as he slid over for the try that put an exclamation point on the victory and clinched his honour of being named the Lance Todd Trophy winner for the player of the match chosen by the press. That announcement was made just after Briers kicked the ball off after Leeds' last try. It is hard to imagine Briers looking more delighted had his own name been announced and the high-five between him and Hodgson is just a glimpse of the excellent team spirit in the side.

If I was a Super League official I think at times I would be tempted to ask for a massive pay rise, because if you listen to so many fans after a game you would think that they have far more influence over the result of the game than any of the players or coaches. The Leeds fans griped about Delaney's disallowed try and the 'knock-on' by Briers, conveniently forgetting about Ratchford's disallowed try after Westwood's 'knock-on', the harsh penalty against Carvell that led to Leeds' first try, the equally harsh penalty for dragging into touch, the call against Briers for obstruction that could have gone either way and the most baffling one of all when Peacock was so far from square at the play-the-ball that any further and he would have been in Warrington's line and yet when Monaghan ran into him and was tackled by him there was no penalty. People never remember the calls that go against the winners.

Officials in any sport have an incredibly tough job and I think rugby league is one of the tougher ones, and they consistently make fewer mistakes than the players. After years of bemoaning the luck of the top teams like St Helens and Wigan, it is the most blissful of music to my ears anytime I hear another fan describe Wire as lucky, you never call a rubbish side lucky.

Final score: Wire 35 Leeds 18

Round 26 v Huddersfield (home) – 2nd September 2012

AS THE league season is drawing to a close and virtually all eyes are already on the play-offs, this performance had so many aspects to it that summed up the season so far. This time the 20-minute spell of brilliance came in the last quarter of the game, Huddersfield being blown away by quick play and some brilliant tries. There were also too many handling errors from Wire, not for the first time this season. Defensively it was one of the most dominant displays of the campaign, such was the aggression at times that they actually looked like they were attacking even when Huddersfield had the ball.

There were several sets where the Giants barely made ten metres, and all of this with a few key players missing, as has so often been the case this year. The final trait of the season that was on display in this game was that once again Wire did more than enough to win.

Throughout the match Warrington looked the better side, but for around half an hour or so at least it looked like having the potential to turn into one of those silly games that end up a lot closer than they should be. This was due mainly to the frequency of the handling errors form Wire.

Myler and Ratchford already have the makings of an excellent half-back partnership with Myler growing into the role of team organiser and helping take them forward, while Ratchford always looks likely to create something out wide. Both of them have that trait of all excellent half-backs that they come alive inside the opponents' 20-metre area, taking the responsibility to help their team gain the most difficult yards of all and cross the try-line.

Whichever personnel make up the pack we can be sure that they are not going to be bullied or dominated. The chances are it will be them doing the bullying let alone holding their own. The team's bunch of 'piano carriers' do their job at least as well as any other pack in Super League, shifting those pianos around at great speed and putting them in great position for the team's 'piano players' like Hodgson, Briers, Myler and Ratchford to show their skills. You would always want Briers in your side, but this was one of those performances when you didn't particularly notice he was missing. I do feel the team struggle when both him and Hodgson are missing, that vital ingredient of composure being taken away.

Some of the tries produced in this game were a throwback to the Harlem Globetrotter days earlier in the season; the offloads and quick passes were more frequent than of late. The champagne moment for me would be Hodgson's one-handed tip-on pass to Williams to set up his try in the left corner. No doubt that style of play increases the entertainment factor, but I also think it could well be a factor in the play-offs if Wire find themselves looking to make a breakthrough in a tight game or come from behind late on in a match.

Wigan coach Sean Wane claims that the trophy he wanted most this season was the League Leader's Shield. While I agree that finishing top is an achievement to be proud of, to say it's the most important of the three trophies available is like a kid at Christmas seeing a PlayStation, an iPhone and a pencil case under the tree, then claiming that it was the pencil case he wanted most when his brother and sister get the PlayStation and iPhone. Warrington already have one of the two big prizes available and will go after the other one from second position. Here's hoping that, like those Olympic match sprint cyclists, being second will be an advantage for Wire and they will be in the perfect place to attack from.

Final score: Wire 54 Huddersfield 6

Round 27 v Widnes (away) – 9th September 2012

IS IT really round 27 already? All the league games played and the season seems to have flown by, but I doubt it has gone so fast for all the players. With nothing tangible at stake we knew the changes to the line-up were coming and most of us probably feared that a repeat of the sort of performance that was produced at Salford and London, not so much because we thought it was a distinct possibility, but that we really didn't want to have a performance like that against Widnes.

Any sort of defeat to Widnes would have been even more embarrassing than those two hammerings because of the local derby factor. Instead, not for the first time, making many changes to the team still resulted in a thoroughly professional performance and a more than sound win.

Having completed a half-marathon in the morning – I use the word completed rather than ran, because I only ran the first 100 yards or so before feeling a muscle pull in my calf and then walked the rest of the way – I decided to forgo the short trip to Widnes and settle for listening to the game on the radio as I lay in bed recovering. I must admit that I dozed off to sleep a couple of times, even a brisk walk of that distance is clearly enough to wear me out. However I heard more than enough to know that Wire had produced another display full of creativity, desperation in defence and that wonderful ability to score tries.

I was reminded of a time when a disgruntled Liverpool fan turned to me after a Manchester United goal had been scored as we watched it on the TV and said: "That's all you're good at, scoring goals." I simply nodded, smiled and replied: "That's a pretty good thing to be good at though." All sports have a scoring system and many things can be an influence on that score, but ultimately the act of scoring itself along with the ability to stop your opponents scoring is always going to be the most important ability.

The Widnes player working as a co-commentator on Wire FM made a few references to things he had been watching on video about Warrington's performance. He had to acknowledge that there was a world of difference between knowing what was coming and being able to stop it. It is noticeable that when Warrington are attacking close to their opponents' line, they look similar to every other team in Super League in terms of the way they set up and the options they want to take. The big difference is that they do those things much better than most. Most great teams in any sport throughout history haven't done anything different, they have merely done the same things better than anyone else.

Now the jockeying for position is complete, all that remains is the four-week hunt for ultimate glory that is the play-offs. We know we will enter from second place, meaning home field advantage throughout the play-offs, provided we win our first game. That first match is a tough one against St Helens, the only team to beat us at home this year. A win will give us a week off before the semi-final and a defeat will give us another chance to win a home game to get a place in the final four. It can all get confusing when you are trying to explain it to someone, but essentially, if we keep winning we will be champions, if we keep losing we won't.

About halfway through the season I named a 17 that I would select had the Grand Final been the following week. Since then a few people have played themselves into my 17, and a few therefore have played their way out, either due to not being on their best form, not playing much since then or just being unlucky enough to have someone playing a little bit better in my opinion. For the record my 17 would now be as follows:

Hodgson
Joel Monaghan
Ratchford.
Atkins
Riley
Briers
Myler
Hill
Michael Monaghan
Carvell
Westwood
Waterhouse
Grix
Higham
Morley
Harrison
Bridge

It is still an unbelievably difficult task, but it's great that I am leaving people out who I think deserve to be and are good enough to be in a Grand Final 17, rather than having to pick some who I don't think are good enough.

This is it then, what the whole season has been building towards. Three consecutive wins will see the Wire finally be champions again.

Final score: Widnes 14 Wire 52

Chapter 22

The Play-Offs

SPORT IS about finding out who is the best. But what is the best way to find out who is the best? In 1998 it was decided that the best rugby league team in Europe would be decided by a play-off series, culminating in one 'Grand' Final. Rugby league, although started in England, has been excelled at more in Australia, resulting in the English game unashamedly using many pieces of Australian jargon and finals in Australia are always 'Grand'.

Contrary to what Sky Sports would like you to believe, play-offs are nothing new. Play-offs followed by a championship final were used in rugby league in England long before the Sky 'revolution'. In the 1903/04 season Bradford FC were crowned champions after the play-offs and there wasn't a television camera anywhere to be seen, let alone a high definition one.

Then from 1907 through to 1973, save a couple of years in the 1960s, the champions were the team that won the end-of-season play-offs. To Americans and Australians, who love and embrace play-offs, the concept of an end-of-season finale probably seems like the only way to decide the champions.

To a generation of rugby league fans in this country who had only known the football way of determining things – whoever finishes top after every team has played each other twice – the rebirth of the play-offs in 1998 caused several distrusting murmurings and many grumbles about the unfairness of it all.

The search for ultimate fairness in sport is always likely to be in vain, because sport, being the great metaphor for life that it is, isn't fair. As long as everybody knows at the start of the season how the champions are going to be determined, and nothing changes over the course of that season, then that is as fair as you can ask for.

Is the top of the table system fair? If Manchester United and Manchester City are going head to head for the title, is it fair that the outcome is decided by results against other teams? Over the course of the season one of the title contenders could play a lot more 'in-form' teams than the other. One contender could have to play at somewhere like Wigan on a freezing cold day in February, when Wigan are scrapping to avoid relegation. The other contender could play them on a beautiful sunny day in May, with Wigan's Premiership future already assured and the players' bodies at the DW Stadium but their minds in the Bahamas.

On the all too rare occasion that the football title is decided on the last day of the season, it is almost unheard of for the two title rivals to be going head to head. So there could be a scenario where United will be champions if they win at home to an already relegated team at the bottom of the table, and City only manage a draw away to a team who need a point to clinch a top four spot. That would be like the heavyweight champion of the world drawing his bout but losing his belt because on the same day another contender beat a journeyman pro convincingly inside three rounds. Fair?

The ludicrously named Champions League is regarded as the biggest, most prestigious club competition in the world, and certainly the competition any club in Europe would most like to win. Teams from all over Europe are split into little groups, then the top two from each group make up the last 16 teams, who then take part in a straight knockout competition until the winner is identified. That's beginning to sound suspiciously like a play-off system is good enough for the biggest prize in European football.

In 1989 when the English football championship was decided by the two challengers playing each other in the last match of the season, football fans were delighted with the exciting prospect of the title being decided in that fashion. That night Arsenal had to beat Liverpool by two clear goals at Anfield to take the title away from Liverpool and the fact that they did so, with a goal in the last minute, afforded the match complete legendary status.

Imagine every season coming down to the last game with the two title contenders playing each other, then you have imagined the play-offs. Another advantage of the play-offs is that everybody knows well in advance exactly when the title will be decided, and it quickly becomes established as a permanent fixture in the sporting calendar. One reason for the Super Bowl being the most watched one-day sports event in the world is because we know that it's going be on a Sunday, either in late January or early February, every single year. On this side of the Atlantic we know watching it will mean staying up well past midnight.

This regularity allows fans to look forward to it every year and make plans to make an event out of it. We also know we are going to see two exceptional teams playing each other for the ultimate prize. One group of players will live out their greatest dream, the other group will be left distraught, with their dreams in tatters. That is the glorious drama of sport.

One of the qualities we tend to admire most in our sports stars is the ability to get the job done when it matters most. We won't remember Jack Nicklaus for his wins in the Philadelphia Golf Classic, or the Sahara Invitational, we will remember him for his 18 professional Major championships and his almost superhuman ability to peak for the big occasion. In years to come we won't be reminiscing about Roger Federer's wins in Milan and Rotterdam, we will remember the triumphs in Paris and Melbourne and the domination in New York and Wimbledon.

Play-offs provide team sports stars with the opportunity to show just how good they really are. A big reason as to why Michael Jordan is widely acknowledged as the greatest basketball player ever is that of the six times he won the NBA Championship with the Chicago Bulls he was named Most Valuable Player of the series on every occasion. If the game was down to the last few ticks of the clock and the Bulls found themselves a point behind, there was no doubt whose hands they wanted the ball in. Once the ball got into Jordan's hands it would be one of those glorious goose-pimple moments that watching greatness at great moments can provide. Bulls fans weren't hoping he would score, they were expecting he would score. It would be like watching an episode of *Columbo*, you knew who was going to win, you were only watching to find out exactly how he would do it. Then there would be that glorious swish sound, the ball not even touching the sides as it went through the hoop to determine the outcome of the game.

Joe Montana and Tom Brady are revered as the two great quarterbacks of the modern era in American football, not for the numbers and statistics they racked up over the years, but because of their cold-blooded performances in the play-offs where they were able to perform at their best when it mattered most, time and time again. Would we ever have known just how great players like this were or are, if their teams were winning titles by finishing a few points clear of the other teams after a long season?

Besides, when every season ends with two top teams bashing hell out of each other in front of 75,000 at Old Trafford, in a match of immense intensity that could well be decided by a last-minute score, who wants fair? It is fitting that the drama of having one game to decide who rules them all is played out at the 'Theatre of Dreams'.

Chapter 23

Last Year's Play-Offs

LOVE THEM or loathe them, and as I've already alluded to plenty of people are in both camps, it looks a certainty that the play-offs are going to be how Super League champions are decided for at least the foreseeable future. Last season's play-offs started slowly, but in the end they provided the drama and the story that the game has been waiting for since the play-offs came back in 1998.

It was Warrington themselves that got the play-offs started with a 47-0 drubbing of Huddersfield, an utterly dominant performance that guaranteed a home semi-final, having the 'club call' and that fans' expectations would remain sky high. In the other qualifying play-off Saints provided the first upset of the series by winning at Wigan, to book their passage to the semi-finals.

Both the elimination play-offs turned out to be hopelessly one-sided affairs which sadly back up those beliefs that the competition isn't strong enough to justify eight teams making the end-of-season contest. Seventh-placed Hull KR were battered in France by Catalans and eighth-placed Hull were equally soundly beaten at Leeds.

Wigan and Huddersfield were afforded a second chance the following week, Wigan took theirs, Huddersfield didn't. Catalans' performance the week before had people thinking that they could trouble Wigan but as it happened it was their turn to be on the wrong end of a lopsided scoreboard. Leeds went to Huddersfield and looked to be continuing their well-timed run at the end of the season with another comfortable win and serene performance until a thrilling fightback by the Giants in the last few minutes left Leeds looking vulnerable and more like the team that had struggled through the first 20 weeks or so of the season. Somehow they managed to hang on, Huddersfield's comeback ultimately coming up one try short of the miracle. Leeds' late wobble just turned out to be one more reason for Wire fans' expectations to be cruelly raised.

Then came the semi-finals, first of all that thrilling game in Warrington where Leeds played like champions, arguably for the first time all season, just when they needed to most. Saints were equally impressive in managing to beat Wigan for the second time in three weeks. This produced the slightly paradoxical state of two underdogs reaching the Grand Final, the same two teams that contested three of the last four finals, and Saints making their sixth consecutive Grand Final appearance.

Leeds produced another performance worthy of champions on the biggest stage of all, winning the title for the fourth time in five years. Saints performed well, but not quite well enough, losing the final for the fifth time in a row. Their bridesmaid outfit is beginning to look old, and they just can't seem to be the one who grabs the bouquet.

This was the season that the Super League executives had been waiting for, one where all four semi-finalists were more than capable of being the champions and Huddersfield had been extremely competitive at the top of the table for two thirds of the season. Most of the previous Super League seasons had only produced two genuine challengers for the title at the most.

Leeds winning from fifth has breathed new life into the whole play-off concept. If they didn't know it already teams have now seen the benefit of scrapping your way into the play-offs on the back of an average season. As a rugby league fan I was glad the bold idea to bring back the play-offs had been justified by the excitement of both semi-finals, the final and the great story of former champions Leeds proving that they still have what it takes to win the big one. As a Warrington fan I was of course left thinking: "Did it have to be this year?"

Chapter 24

Sporting Curses Broken – England Win Cricket's Ashes in 2005

I HAVE vague memories of David Gower scoring a double hundred in 1985, and of watching highlights on a small black and white television of England's win in Australia in the 1986/87 series. Other than those fleeting memories all I had witnessed was a defeat every two years, many of which had been hopelessly one-sided hammerings, all the way up to the 2005 Ashes.

In the build-up to that series we had tried to convince ourselves that this time would be different, without too much success. Despite England being ranked number two in the world, they were still way behind the all-conquering Australians, and the fact that England had developed a new ruthless streak under captain Michael Vaughan we still couldn't truly believe that we would beat the Australians. As the games got closer and the build-up more intense we got caught up in it again, thinking that maybe with home advantage we could somehow manage a series win.

The first day of the series was an explosive start, a sign of things to come, when England unbelievably ripped through the much vaunted Australian batting, bowling them out for a paltry 190 in front of a packed house at Lord's. Just when we were daring to dream the impossible dream, we were woken up and then plunged into an all too familiar nightmare as the legendary pace bowler Glenn McGrath hit back in spectacular fashion and we were bundled out for 155. The Aussies went on to secure a 1-0 series lead with a comfortable 239-run win.

After that let-down of a result most of the journalists were scathing in their views on the England team. I still had most of my optimism intact – we had bowled the Aussies out twice, once for a very low score, two things we hardly ever did. Also it looked like we had a batsman who was prepared to take the Aussies on and fight fire with fire in the form of Kevin Pietersen.

Next came possibly the biggest turning point in the series and it happened before the second match even started. McGrath trod on a cricket ball during the warm-up and rolled his ankle, counting him out of the second Test. The Aussies had to go in without the leader of their bowling attack and the best pace bowler in the world. It became a Test that a lot of people consider to be the best ever played. From the moment Australian captain Ricky Ponting won the toss and chose to bowl, shocking everybody, England were in control. They posted over 400 runs in the first innings and scored them in an aggressive style that could easily be described as "Australian-like".

If one over can set the tone for an entire series it was maybe the one Andrew Flintoff bowled at Ponting in the Australian first innings. Every ball was good enough to get him out and one of the best batsmen of all time was left bamboozled by Flintoff before the last ball did indeed dismiss him. England now could see that their best was good enough to beat the Australian best.

Just when England looked to be cruising to a reasonably easy win, the Aussies dug in and their tail-end batsmen started to get closer and closer to the total required to win the match. All of the optimism and positivity that had been created over the previous three days was slipping away with a feeling of "same old England". Then with Australia needing just three runs to win, Harmison bounced one down the leg side and it brushed the glove of the last Aussie batsman. England wicketkeeper Jones gratefully clung on to the winning catch. The fact that close-up replays showed that Kasprowicz had his hand off the bat handle when the ball brushed his glove, meaning that he technically shouldn't have been given out, only served to add to the drama. That the Aussies didn't grumble about the decision was one of the early signs of an excellent spirit between the two sides. It would have been easy for England to crumble to a defeat, but they had stuck to it.

The third match was almost as epic. England surprised most people by continuing their dominance and in this match they were even more in command despite the return of McGrath, but time saved the Aussies on this occasion, with the match ending as a draw thanks to the Australians hanging on with just one wicket left. I was one of thousands left locked out of the ground on that unbelievably tense final day. England clearly had an attack that was capable of bowling out the Australians, something we hadn't been able to say since the mid-1980s. With two matches to go the series was tied at 1-1 and England were undoubtedly in with a chance of an historic victory.

The fourth Test was the third of undoubtedly the three best consecutive Test matches of all time. Once again England took control and put themselves in a strong winning position, needing just 129 in their second innings to win the match and take a 2-1 lead in the series. Surely that would be easy enough, especially as McGrath's ankle had ruled him out of the match again, but the Aussies are nothing if not fighters and the legendary leg-spinner Shane Warne and the nastily aggressive pace bowler Brett Lee started taking wicket after wicket. It started to look like an Australian victory might somehow be snatched, a victory that would see them retain the Ashes. Once again though England managed to settle themselves just in time and tail-enders Giles and Hoggard saw them through to a nail-biting win with three wickets to spare.

One more match remained and England just needed a draw to win back the Ashes for the first time since 1987. England posted a decent total of 373 batting first, but it wasn't nearly enough to put an Aussie victory out of the equation. Leading by six runs after the first innings, but still with plenty of time left in the game, England still had a lot of batting to do during the last day. At 125-6 England once again looked on the brink of collapse, a collapse that so often in the past would have continued and caused them to lose the game. This year was clearly different though, and thanks largely to a brilliant innings of 158 by Kevin Pietersen and a fantastically gritty knock of 59 by Ashley Giles England managed to get up to 335 all out, with barely enough time for the Australians to start their innings, let alone chase down the 342 required for an Ashes-saving victory.

In the middle of the most competitive day of cricket imaginable, there was still time for a brilliant moment of good humoured interaction. Around the time of the resumption of play after a break, there was plenty of cloud around and a stoppage for bad light or rain would have been gratefully accepted by England at the time. Many members of the crowd started putting their umbrellas up in a vain attempt to send a message to the umpires that conditions weren't suitable for play. To their eternal credit every member of the Australian team came back out from the pavilion wearing completely unnecessary sunglasses, to send the opposite signal to the umpires.

England's victory was put into perspective 18 months later when virtually the same Australian team won the Ashes back with a 5-0 whitewash Down Under. In 2005 England had a couple of lucky breaks in the injury to McGrath and the decision to give Kasprowicz out in the second Test match. But they had gone toe to toe with the best team in the world and one of the best ever, over a five-match series of five-day matches, and not only had they squeezed out a victory, they had thoroughly deserved to do so by completely out-playing their higher-ranked opponents for the majority of a series that most if not all cricketing experts would call the greatest ever.

Lesson to be learned from breaking this curse: you might need a little bit of luck to win the big one, but you need to be good enough to take advantage of that luck. Sometimes your opponent might be better than you, but if you stand up to them and take them on in a positive manner with a belief that you can beat them, then you might be better than them when it matters.

Chapter 25

This Year's Play-Offs

AFTER 27 matches (playing each team home and away, plus the Magic Weekend game in Manchester in May), 14 contenders have been whittled down to eight. Over the next three weekends six will be eliminated, then there is that one match to decide the champions.

As a general guide to assess the chances of each of the eight teams it can be useful to look at the bookies' odds. It's completely erroneous to say that bookies don't make any mistakes, but they don't make too many and when they do they don't tend to be too big. Here's a list of the best odds available for each of the play-off teams:

Warrington	11/8
Wigan	13/8
St Helens	9/1
Leeds	14/1
Les Catalans	20/1
Hull FC	60/1
Huddersfield	100/1
Wakefield	250/1

So it would appear that the bookies think it is essentially a two-horse race between Wire and the Pie Eaters. They did think exactly the same last year and the final ended up being played out between Leeds and St Helens. Once again the bookies see them as the greatest threat, but don't seem all that confident that lightning can strike twice. Both have such a phenomenal record of reaching Old Trafford in recent times though that until somebody knocks them out of the play-offs, there will always be more than a nagging feeling that they might just make it there again.

Catalans are definitely the liveliest of the outsiders, but are probably a little too reliant on home advantage to become champions. Hull are capable of pulling off an upset, but they will need three to become champions and that does seem highly unlikely. Huddersfield have once again made Devon Loch look like a fast-finishing fourth, as they spent some time up at the top of the table, only to collapse in the second half of the season and slump to seventh. Wakefield have done completely the opposite, winning the last seven games to make it into the play-offs from a position that looked hopeless. One way or another, neither team look strong enough to make an argument for the league being strong enough in depth to justify having as many as eight teams in the play-offs.

The first game of this year's play-offs saw Catalans travel to Wigan and ultimately put in a very disappointing performance. Of all the top teams in the top four I would say those first round matches were most important for Catalans. Wigan, St Helens and Warrington are better equipped to shrug off a bad performance and turn in a better one next week, but more to the point a win at Wigan would have guaranteed Catalans a home semi-final. The other three are almost as likely to win on their travels as they are to win at home, especially when playing each other, whereas Catalans' chances of winning a semi-final would be greatly increased if they were playing on their own ground. So that made their somewhat timid performance surprising. It left Wigan in their element, bullying a side down the middle and then taking advantage of the space that created out wide for their evasive runners. Ultimately it all added up to a big win for Wigan.

The two knockout games of the first round produced the results that most people were expecting. Defending champions Leeds beat Wakefield, but not before Wakefield backed up their end-of-season form with an impressively spirited performance, and had one pass gone to hand after a break late in the game then they might well have gone on to produce a big upset win. Huddersfield couldn't magically summon up a good performance after a string of poor ones, and never looked like beating Hull.

Chapter 26
Match Reports

Play-offs first round v St Helens (home) – 15th September 2012

SO THAT'S what a lead balloon going down sounds like. For about an hour it threatened to turn into a classic play-off tussle, two top teams in a closely fought contest. Both teams had managed to create one try each and the difference on the scoreboard was there because Warrington had gifted St Helens another try and they had given nothing in return. In the back of my mind was the thought that Wire hadn't had their trademark burst of 15-20 minutes that has so often been the difference in matches this season, when they score three or four unanswered tries. It either never materialised or Saints managed to withstand it.

Early in the second half Wire did crank up the pressure and had several attacks on the Saints' line. We were waiting for the floodgates to open and they did, only at the other end. An excellent break by Lomax down the Saints' right led to a try that not only saw the end to Warrington's period of pressure, but turned out to be the first of a few St Helens tries as they started to rack up the points.

In a way the Wire tasted their own medicine, in that the game throughout was very even if you just watched the action to both 20-metre lines. This was one of the very rare occasions where Wire were outplayed at both ends of the pitch. St Helens defended their line with great enthusiasm and organisation, and gradually picked holes in Warrington's goal line defence.

I honestly think the spirit was still in the Wire team, seeing them celebrate keeping St Helens out in the South-East corner late on in the first half as if they had just scored a match-winning try was a glaring example of that. They would support each other after they made a mistake and congratulate each other after doing something good. It was simply a case that too many of them had a bad day. Many of the crowd seemed to be getting on their backs at the end and lots of the handling errors came when they were chasing the game.

One thing for sure with this team is that they will try to do whatever they think gives them the best chance to win the game, even if they know there is a great chance that option will result in them suffering a bigger defeat and some embarrassment. Personally I prefer that to a team who plays out the percentages, with no true intention of winning, just so they can save face. One day they will pull off a miracle come-from-behind victory and all those extra margins of defeat will be worth it.

It's amazing how one bad performance can destroy the optimism of so many fans around me. Three Challenge Cup wins in four years, finishing in the top three in the league for the last three years and consistently beating their main rivals over the last two years seemed to have been all forgotten in the space of a few minutes. Instead some people have decided to focus on play-off failures in previous seasons. Unfortunately it does seem to be the case that most humans' default setting is for negativity and pessimism. Hopefully the players and coaches don't share this setting.

Now the team is staring down the barrel of being stuck with one of the labels any sports star least wants, a "choker". To suggest a team or an individual doesn't perform their best when it matters is one of the deepest cuts a sports star can receive because it fundamentally goes against everything about them that makes them so competitive. From previous seasons Wire already have this reputation from fans of other clubs and maybe a few of their own fans.

What they have to remember is reputations can change. In his early days Nick Faldo had a reputation for letting golf tournaments slip through his fingers, so much so that the American press began to label him "Foldo". By the end of his career he had made a mockery of that name and was universally acknowledged as one of the great pressure players of all time. As a young player Roger Federer got the reputation of being a talented player without the mental toughness to win a Grand Slam championship, but so far he has proved that farcical assessment wrong on 17 occasions. Manchester United undoubtedly choked in trying to win the league title in 1992 and they could have continued to play the role of chokers as they looked for their first title in 26 years. Instead they became the team that all others feared being around the lead towards the end of a season. On the last day of the 2011/12 football season Manchester City looked like living up to their reputation of being a joke club one more time, until two goals in stoppage time fought the huge weight of history and started to build a new reputation. In rugby league until the last few years Leeds were known as the 'glamorous' big city club that would virtually never win the championship. Their modern-day players had to battle to create a new reputation, and now they are the team that all the others desperately want to see eliminated from the play-offs.

Reputations come about from actions, and actions can change and actions are under your control. The good news from Saturday night's game was that Wire picked the best day in the play-offs to have a bad day. Players need to think how bad that defeat felt and times it by about a thousand to imagine how bad an elimination from the play-offs will feel. They can take their feelings from winning the Challenge Cup and times them by about ten to imagine how good it will feel to win the ultimate prize at Old Trafford, a prize that so many are saying they are not capable of winning.

The situation hasn't changed too much from last week – Wire still need to win three consecutive games to be champions. Now they have to set about building a new reputation, starting with next weekend's home game, hopefully played out in front of a full house of supportive fans. Ending 57 years of pain was never going to be easy. No destination truly worth getting to has an easy journey to get there. You have to believe before you can achieve.

Final score: Wire 6 St Helens 28

IN A way the play-offs are quite simple now. Wire are in a quarter-final against Hull, the winners go into the semi-finals and losers are done. This is the first match all season that I've been genuinely nervous about, simply because it is the first match all season that can end their chance to be champions – no more second chances. Even before the cup games I had a calm confidence about me, maybe because I had seen them win it before, just two and three years ago. Now I am completely conflicted. On the one hand I have faith in this group of players to believe in themselves enough to perform when it matters most. On the other hand last week's defeat was a stark reminder that this is still Warrington we are talking about and

Warrington, play-offs and winning championships just don't seem to mix.

While the opponents aren't the strongest team in Super League they are a good side in good form and one that is always capable of beating a top team. Also they are a ghost from the past. Hull were the club that started this whole curse back in 1956, as well as being the ones that burst our Andrew Johns balloon in 2005. Both of those Hull victories were ones that came on our own patch.

My confident self can envision us tearing Hull to pieces with Michael Monaghan and Mickey Higham leading the pack to utter dominance down the middle and our backs being too classy for them and racking up the points. The pundits will say that there is a gulf in class between Warrington, Wigan, Saints, Leeds and the rest and that last week was just a poor day for Wire. My pessimistic, seen all the disappointments before, self can already hear the boos from the crowd and the look of dejection and embarrassment on the players' faces as they concede a try late on that clinches a comfortable win for Hull.

Then there's the sadistic thrill-seeking self who wants a disappointing performance to start with, followed by a rousing comeback that is capped off by a try off the last play of the game that takes us from two points behind, to two points in front, with the chaotic scenes of celebration in the ground followed by the greatly increased belief that finally this is our year.

This is definitely the sort of game you would rather be playing in rather than watching as this feeling of not being able to do anything to affect the result is not a good one to have. You can kid yourself that following rituals and having positive thoughts will make all the difference, but you know it won't. Maybe my article on the *Guardian* website after the Saints game would have a positive effect on the players, if any of them read it. Again I could well be kidding myself. One way or another we will know by the end of tonight's game, either we live to fight another day and are just two wins away from the ultimate prize, or we have suffered a devastating, soul-destroying, dream-crushing loss.

Play-offs second round v Hull (home) – 22nd September 2012

THE DREAM is still alive, the quest for both ultimate glory and the complete 80-minute performance is still in progress. From the start it looked like the emphasis all week had been on defence, Wire determined to be solid and dominating when they didn't have the ball. Handling errors did still occur, but at least none of them resulted in tries for the opposition this week. The better your defence is the more you can get away with handling errors.

I remember watching big play-off games in years gone by, between top teams when Warrington's dreams for the year had long since died, and what always struck me was that it was the defence of the two teams on show that was where they were so much better than Warrington. Now that Wire have the organisation and much more importantly the desire to defend well for 80 minutes, they always have a chance of beating anybody, anywhere.

If they have learned anything from this game I hope it's that they don't have to force tries to happen as soon as they get beyond their opponents' 20-metre line. The first try came about when they used up all their tackles on Hull's line, then an excellent kick from Briers and an enthusiastic chase resulted in a score for Waterhouse. Myler's try followed, when Wire had switched the ball from left to right, stretching Hull's defence to breaking point, the result being a chasm of a gap for Myler to run through as the ball was moved back to the left.

In the second half a bit of magic from Ratchford in broken play created a try out of nothing. Then a simple, well supported break down the middle created the final try for Hodgson. Obviously none of these tries would have happened had they lost the ball, looking for a miracle pass, earlier in those sets. Wire have to back themselves to score enough tries to win any game if they consistently give themselves six chances to score whenever they get inside their opponents' 20-metre line.

With Briers' kicking game, Hodgson's creativeness out wide and several dangerous runners Warrington are at least as well equipped as any team to turn territorial pressure into points. Clearly now we are at the business end of the season I am not quite so keen to fully support the cavalier Harlem Globetrotter style of play that I championed so much earlier in the year. I must be getting nervous!

This was a composed performance that went some way to putting paid to the theory that Warrington will always bottle it in the play-offs. Hull were gradually ground down and they never looked like winning, despite displaying a strong spirit themselves and being backed by a passionate following. Composure and patience were on display from Wire, but that's not to say that there weren't any trademark offloads. There were some really good offloads, the sort where the ball carrier is in complete control of the ball and the supporting player is expecting the ball, so the more of those type of offloads definitely the better.

Other than not being at their slick best in attack, this was an impressive Wire performance in a match that truly mattered. The most worrying thing about the attack was the signs of hesitancy when moving the ball wide near Hull's line, as if they weren't convinced they were taking the best option and that their timing with each other was a little off. Maybe they are saving the two best performances for last. Another worrying sign is the knocks and injuries are starting to mount up a little. Michael Monaghan and Briers are probably the two players we would least want to do without, so seeing them both down injured for a while was not good, then late on Myler, whose late season good form continues, also went down injured. Hopefully Westwood and Carvell will be back for the semi-final as they have both been missed. However, the positive way to look at it is that there is no such thing as injury problems, only opportunities for other players to shine.

So we are not playing our best, picking up a few injuries, have a reputation for losing our nerve in the play-offs, Leeds are defending champions, play-off experts and in good form and they have had an extra day's rest compared to Warrington. Yet despite all this Wigan still chose to play Leeds. We can't be doing too badly.

Two wins, just two more wins from everything the players, coaches and fans have dreamed of. Firstly we have to go to St Helens where it will be either repeat or revenge. Over the course of the season I have made reference to a song from Kelly Clarkson and one from Journey, and now it's time for a bit of Lady Gaga – Edge of Glory.

Final score: Wire 24 Hull 12

Chapter 27
The Last Chance

Play-off semi-final v Saints (away) – 29th September 2012

I BUY my ticket from the club shop on Tuesday, then start wondering whether floods are going to have an effect on the game. Will the venue be switched? It turns out that was just my imagination running away with me. As the week goes by the nerves start to hit me, I can't remember being this nervous before a game. Before the Challenge Cup semi-final in 2009 against Wigan I still had the "happy to be there" mentality, along with expecting the worst, so my hopes weren't high enough to create these sorts of nerves. Only in the second half of that game, with Wire threatening to throw away a big lead, did the butterflies start to take over. Before the final that year I can remember being strangely confident we were going to beat Huddersfield. As the game panned out I really couldn't see how we could lose it and the fact that meant we would win the Challenge Cup was a constant source of confusion in my head throughout the second half.

The nerves I am feeling now are as if I am standing in the tunnel about to go and play. I think the play-offs bring that extra sense of tingling compared to the cup, because if you lose you know your entire season is over, you have to win to get to play another game. I picture being at the match any time I get a spare moment or too without any distractions. Even when I have the strong distraction of watching the Ryder Cup on TV I still have moments where I'm envisaging the action being played out before me at Langtree Park. Maybe it's because I have invested so much into writing this book that I have got such a state of nerves. From a selfish point of view I have an added reason for not wanting them to lose tonight – it would ruin my book!

My mum was running a business training course this week from the Halliwell Jones Stadium and she said she could have stayed looking at the pictures from seasons gone by for hours. On the Friday the players were out on the pitch training. It sounded like there was a Usain Bolt-like relaxation about the session, but I am sure that's what they need the day before the biggest game of the season so far.

On the Friday night I watch Wigan v Leeds on TV in the other semi-final and it does nothing to cool my excitement and nerves. It's a classic play-off clash, even Wigan fans wouldn't have left before the end, with Leeds somehow finding their way to Old Trafford again via a late – but thankfully not at all controversial – penalty giving them a 13-12 victory. How many times does a team have to do it before it's not a surprise anymore? Now we have to hope that the other team that are experts at getting to Old Trafford don't book yet another meeting with Leeds at the Theatre of Dreams. Saints are bidding for their seventh consecutive Grand Final place but they have lost on the last five occasions. Surely nobody in rugby league wants them turning up again like an uncle at a wedding who nobody really wants there.

On the afternoon of the game I go and visit an old friend up in Eccleston and she has no interest in rugby league whatsoever, which was probably good for stopping me obsessing about the game. I manage to find my way from there to St Helens in time for the game, park in a multi-storey car park and end up on the top floor. I can only imagine how long it's going to take to get out of there at the end of the game, but I really don't care about then, by this stage all I'm thinking about is the game itself.

I got to the ground just before 6pm and the first thing I was hoping for was a good turnout from Wire fans, but I didn't seem to be walking past too many of them. As soon as I got to the terraces, I realised why I hadn't walked past too many of them, they were virtually all in the ground already. It was great to see the packed out terraces behind the sticks, so packed that for a while I thought I was going to struggle to find a spot to stand. That was a fantastic, uplifting start to the evening.

Right from the start it looked clear to me that Wire were going to put in a good performance, and all that remained to be seen was whether it would be good enough. The first half was a close tussle. I felt like Warrington were the better side, but not quite able to assert any dominance. From our viewpoint on the terraces it felt like a lot of close calls were going against us and that resulted in Wire having to defend their line more than they would have liked to.

It is often the case though that when you go to watch the match you can get caught up in the groans from the fans around you and be led to believe that your team is being hard done to, more so than if you sat at home and watched it on TV. Saints were clearly up for the fight and looked sharp in attack. The great desire to defend their line that Warrington have shown so many times this year was put to the test. Saints did produce three tries in that first half, but they had to do it via two expert finishes right in the corner and one extremely awkward spiral bomb.

They didn't get anything easy and Warrington's defence had stood up to the storm more than well enough to keep them in the game.

In attack Warrington looked sharp themselves. A trademark handling movement created a try for Riley in the corner as the ball was passed from Briers to Myler and then to Hodgson. It was a move we had seen so many times so far this season, the accuracy of the passes and the timing and angle of the runs by Waterhouse and Atkins going through the Saints line, creating plenty of space for Hodgson to be able to send Riley racing over with another accurate pass. It was so good to see the execution of the move being close to perfect just when we needed it most.

Just when it looked like Saints would go it at half-time with a 14-6 lead, Grix showed exactly how you are meant to run on to the ball with the belief that you will make the try-line and nobody will stop you. The lead-up to that try was another piece of trademark Wire brilliance. It all started when Myler scooped up a grubber kick from Lomax near the Wire try-line and from there he raced away, getting to around the halfway line before being hauled down. From there a succession of offloads created havoc in the Saints defence and they were unable to scramble adequately enough to stop Grix. The ever reliable Hodgson kicked both the goals and that meant they only trailed by two points going in at half-time.

As soon as the first half ended, I got another uplifting sight. The Wire players didn't trudge off, disappointed with being behind, or chat pointlessly to the referee to question certain decisions, instead they ran off and more importantly they ran off together. Speaking to a St Helens fan later in the week he said that when he saw "your lot" run off the pitch like that, he had turned to his mate and said: "We're in trouble here." He felt that Saints had thrown everything at them, including the kitchen sink and that it hadn't been enough.

After what seemed like an even longer than normal half-time break, Warrington let a kick bounce near their line, but thankfully Atkins and Hodgson scrambled across to bundle Makinson into touch. From then the second half settled into an 'arm wrestle', with both teams jostling for territory and neither one making any major mistakes. Hodgson showed his mental toughness by safely gathering a towering bomb under all sorts of pressure, especially impressive after his mistake in the first half.

Gradually Warrington's slight superiority in defence and strength of running started to make a difference. A poor kick was returned by Joel Monaghan to close to the halfway line. Starting a set from there I felt that Wire should at least be in position to put in an attacking kick on the last tackle. Indeed they did exactly that, and Briers produced one of his pinpoint accurate chip kicks, Joel Monaghan one of his perfectly timed jumps and along with a ricochet, that was enough to produce the try that gave Wire a lead they would never surrender. Among all the debate as to whether it was a try or not was probably lost just how impressive a skill it was for Monaghan to scoop up a moving ball with one hand, while he was on his knees. It would have been so easy to knock that ball on.

Now it was the stage of the match where Warrington were in the ascendancy. They had a similar spell in the first round of the play-offs against Saints but in that match Saints not only came out of that spell unscathed, they also ended it with a breakaway try of their own. In the game that really mattered, Warrington showed the required composure, quality and belief to turn pressure into points. Waterhouse crashed over for two tries, continuing his strong form at the end of the season. Earlier on in the year I had suggested he wasn't quite deserving of his place in the 17, but now he is producing performances that have more than justified his selection, a constant threat in attack whether he gets the ball or not, and more importantly he seems to have improved his defence within the team unit.

Riley then produced another expert finish in the corner and we were jumping up and down in joyous celebration once again. We would look at the updated scoreboard and the time left on the clock and be thinking: "Not even Saints can beat us from here, can they?" This Wire team is way too good to be troubled by any sort of Saints hoodoo; that was crushed along with the destruction of Knowsley Road.

Saints threw everything at us, and we threw it right back in their face. Wire are heading to their first championship final match since 1961, looking for that first title since 1955. Before you go to get your tickets, ask around to see if any of your friends from Warrington want to go, even if they've never watched a rugby match before. This is a massive day for the town as a whole. I'm sure there's plenty of room in Old Trafford for all the genuine fans and a few extras.

One match away, just one match away from everything we've ever wanted. Going up against the Grand Final masters and defending champions Leeds, who have won four of the last five Grand Finals and will not want to give up their title without an almighty fight. When it comes to play-off time they seem to be able to find a way to keep a match close, then somehow produce something to come up with the win. Hopefully they will have a little inferiority complex from our last two Wembley hammerings of them, but something tells me that will be outweighed by their utter confidence in their ability to play at Old Trafford on the biggest occasion of all. Like vampires they are at their best at night; all their powers that seem to fade in the Wembley sun are on full display under the night sky in Manchester in October. Leeds will be a tough proposition, Wire will be tougher.

It has been a long road back to a championship final. Many world-class players have been at the club since then. There have been cup wins, seasons when we have been tantalisingly close to being champions, embarrassing losses and years of ridicule for such mediocrity and underachievement. Let's not forget Paul Cullen and his players in the 2002 season who fought their way out of a relegation battle; who knows what would have happened to the club had they gone down that year?

This current team and coaching staff has fought many battles against the weight of history and the perceived nature of this club, and they have won them all. They have proved that Warrington are capable of winning major trophies, that they are capable of finishing top of the league, that they are capable of winning play-off games that truly matter and that Warrington doesn't have to be a joke club for other club's fans to poke fun at. All of those battles have been won and now they just have one more battle to win to end the long, long wait.

Winning at St Helens booked Wire's place at the biggest wedding of the year. Now they need to make sure they are the bride. Old Trafford is no venue to be a bridesmaid.

Final score: St Helens 18 Wire 36

Chapter 28

Sporting Curses Broken – Leeds Rhinos Win The 2004 Grand Final

LEEDS HAVE always been regarded as one of the biggest rugby league clubs around, with only Wigan having strong claims to be bigger. Yet in their first 100 years Leeds had only won three championships. It wasn't until 1961 that they won the title, and successes followed in 1969 and 1972. Even with that one relatively glorious period, three titles wasn't anything like enough of a return to back up their claims to be as big a club as they were supposed to be. Sharing a venue with Yorkshire County Cricket Club meant that Headingley was the sporting centre of Leeds and Yorkshire. The Leeds club had won the Challenge Cup eight times before that first title in 1961. After their 1999 cup triumph at Wembley they had 12 cup wins, but still just those three championships.

In the modern sporting world where counting trophies is the biggest factor most people take into consideration when rating the size of a club, it was getting more than a little farcical for Leeds to claim to be a massive club when after the first eight years of Super League, they still hadn't added to those three titles. In 2004 they entered the season with a talented squad, full of young players who were starting to establish themselves as Super League stars. With a highly rated Australian coach at the helm, expectations were high. They played an expansive, entertaining and creative style and that was good enough to finish top of the league, but of course that by itself wouldn't end the drought. At the time their fierce local rivals Bradford were the play-off experts, a tag that was highlighted by them when they went to Leeds in the play-offs and won to book their place in the Grand Final. Fortunately for Leeds their league position had earned them the right for a second chance in the play-offs. It was a chance that they didn't waste and they booked their rematch with Bradford at Old Trafford.

It was Leeds' first Grand Final since the first Super League one in 1998, and many of the squad were playing in their first final. Bradford had all the Grand Final experience you could ever want, while Leeds were novices in comparison. In the final itself Leeds played with the belief of seasoned veterans and stuck with their style enough to beat the mighty Bulls and end their 32-year wait for a title. That highly rated Australian coach has to take a lot of credit for instilling the players with the belief they could be champions despite all the historical evidence to the contrary. His name is Tony Smith.

Lesson learned from breaking this curse: Tony Smith is a good coach to have when you're battling history.

Chapter 29

The Final Curtain

Grand Final v Leeds (Old Trafford) – 6th October 2012

SO MY book gets its final chapter, all that remains to be seen is whether there's a happy ending or not. The week building up to the final has so much more excitement around the town than the Wembley week, partly because we are a lot more familiar with Wembley, but also because we acknowledge that this is the biggest prize of all and one we haven't won for so long. People at work who I have hardly ever heard talk about rugby are not only talking about it but plenty of them are going to the game. The queue for tickets on Monday afternoon showed just how many people were desperate to be there. Nobody is writing Leeds off, but everybody is excitedly confident and I don't want to think about the devastation we would be feeling if we lose.

I get my ticket on the Tuesday, no queue at all, but most of the tickets are gone so I end up sat in the gods, just like that high-up view I had at Wembley. Two people are coming with me. Daz will be coming over from Dublin again like he did for Wembley, and the other person is Claire who has never been to a game before but got caught up in the sense of history, and hopefully she will be one of several new fans of rugby league that will be produced by the occasion.

Any time I have a quiet moment during the week, thoughts of how the match might play out run through my head. I have been to a few Grand Finals before and just imagining Wire being one of the teams out there is enough for a shiver down the spine. They've had such a good record in the truly big games over the last few years that I feel confident they will perform well. One exception to that record is of course the play-off semi-final defeat to Leeds last season, so that is one of the many reasons for not taking Leeds at all lightly.

In my article for the *Guardian* after the semi-final I referred to Leeds as vampires, because of their tendency to play better at night time. Usually any time there is a pattern of any sort in sport I find myself coming up with a theory to explain it. These theories are usually the sort that I will never be able to prove, but I put enough thought into them to convince at least myself that it has plenty of truth to it. In this case my theory behind Leeds being so good at night time is that they play their home games on a Friday night, so well over half their league matches will be played at night time, including a few away fixtures to other teams who play on Friday or for a live Sky occasion. So they are used to preparing for an evening game, in terms of what time to get out of bed, what to eat for breakfast, what activity to do during the day, what to have for the pre-match meal and exactly when to eat it.

They also become used to performing at the back end of the day and performing under floodlights and a night sky. So when it comes to a usually sunny Wembley and a match kicking off around 3pm, they are not in their comfort zone. Of course I don't think this is the only reason they perform so well in the play-offs, that is largely due to them being a champion team who know how to perform under pressure, but I do wonder if it is a small reason as to why they are so comfortable performing in the night time play-off games.

Warrington of course play their home games on a Sunday afternoon, often in bright sunshine, again maybe that's why they feel so at home at Wembley and until this year have struggled in the play-offs. Or maybe I just have too much spare time on my hands and should leave the theorising to the ancient Greeks.

Another thing I wonder about Leeds over the last couple of years is whether they have stumbled upon an unlikely route to play-off success by finishing fifth in the table. I am not suggesting they did it on purpose in either of the last two years, or that it is the easiest position to get to the Grand Final from, but I do think there are several advantages to attacking the play-offs from that position. In the first round you play the eighth-placed team, by definition the weakest team in the play-offs, and you play them at home. If you have any designs on Old Trafford this game should be a reasonably comfortable way to ease your way into the play-offs and boost your morale. After this you will always play a team that has been beaten the week before, and often it will be the fourth-placed team who have just suffered a confidence-crushing big defeat at the home of the league leaders.

So the fifth-placed team's confidence is in a much better state than their opponents' and this might be more than enough to overcome the home field advantage. A win there sees you into the semi-final, where you will usually be the lowest-ranked team left in, meaning that a lot more often than not you are going to be chosen by the team with the 'club call'. Now all the pressure is on them, being the top team playing at home against a team they have chosen to play.

Also they have had a week off which isn't always a great thing. While the fifth-placed team is building momentum by winning games in consecutive weeks their opponents have been out of action for nearly two weeks and could easily start a little rusty with their timing off. Of course once you are in the final then it doesn't matter how high you finished, there is no advantage to either team. There you go – it's easy to get to the Grand Final from fifth, no wonder Leeds have done it two years in a row!

On the day of the game I open my curtains in the morning and smile as I see the sun shining brightly in a bright blue sky with just the occasional white cloud. It will get dark during the final but it would be great for us if it stays dry, and great for rugby league as well, as dry means passes and offloads. That suits us and makes for an entertaining spectacle for all those neutrals that might be watching one of their first games of rugby league tonight.

As I write a couple of thousand words of this book I am feeling the sort of nerves you would expect if I was playing tonight. My legs won't stay still and I really feel like hitting something. I decide it's best to go to the gym, to release some of this energy and aggression as well as killing some time.

Back from my sprint session at the gym, I now feel ready to go and prepared to do a job if Smithy and the boys need someone to fill in at the last minute. Putting my crazy daydreaming to one side there is the matter of Tony Smith having to choose which 17 players will represent Warrington in their first championship final since 1961. About halfway through the season I started wondering who would be in my Grand Final 17 should Wire make it to Old Trafford. Now the reality is upon us and my 17 does look a bit different.

To remind you of my 17 halfway through the season, here it is:

Hodgson
Joel Monaghan
Ratchford
Atkins
Riley
Briers
O'Brien
Morley
Michael Monaghan
Carvell
Westwood
Grix
Bridge
Higham
Solomona
Hill
Harrison

On the day itself my Grand Final selection would be:

Hodgson
Joel Monaghan
Ratchford.
Atkins
Riley
Briers
Myler
Hill
Higham
Harrison
Westwood
Waterhouse
Grix
Michael Monaghan
Morley
Wood
Cooper

So since the midway point, O'Brien, Bridge, Carvell and Solomona have been taken out, to be replaced by Myler, Waterhouse, Wood and Cooper. O'Brien has done nothing wrong in my eyes and I would be happy to see him playing tonight, but since Myler came back into the team he has been excellent and more than deserves his place at Old Trafford. Solomona was always going to be a wild card selection and in truth he never got back to enough fitness to be worthy of a place in the 17 at the expense of others. Cooper hasn't played all that much this year, but when he has I have always been impressed by his performances and think that this year has been his best so far for the club in terms of his average level of performance.

Leaving Waterhouse out at the halfway stage was probably the most eyebrow-raising selection. Over the last couple of months he has really settled into the team in both defence and attack and now I have no hesitation in putting him in the starting 13. The biggest disappointment over the season for me has been Chris Bridge, who for whatever reason hasn't been close to his best and has looked to be carrying a bit of excess weight as the season has gone on. Maybe he has been playing with an injury, but whatever the reason for his performances, my hunch that Ratchford would ultimately take his spot at right centre has proved to be correct.

I had put Bridge down at loose forward, a role that I think suits his all-round skills. But now I definitely think Grix deserves that role more. I am only leaving Carvell out because of the question marks over his recent injury, but Paul Wood is more than deserving of his place. Another who could count himself unlucky to not make the final cut would be McCarthy, he could easily get the nod ahead of the likes of Cooper and Harrison.

It really was a grand day out. I saw three lads I went to primary and high school with, two by design and one by good luck. It was that sort of day, the sort of day for us to come together and celebrate something we had waited so long for. We were finally at the Theatre of Dreams, something that only four years ago looked like nothing more than a dream. I was behind the sticks at the Wire end, and being pretty high up gave us a great view of the action and of the rest of the Warrington contingent. If it hadn't quite dawned on us that our team were about to contest a Grand Final, I think the loud crack of the fireworks followed by seeing the two teams emerge from the tunnel left us in no doubt what we were about to witness. I know the occasion created at least one new Wire fan, my friend Claire, who came along to her first ever game. I am hoping there were several more.

Warrington started so well. After having to defend two consecutive Leeds sets courtesy of a harsh verdict of a charged-down kick, Wire produced an excellent set themselves, Higham and Grix in particular making excellent ground with scoots down the middle. The set ended with Briers having the ball in his hands just 20 metres or so away from the Leeds line and he floated over a teasing kick to the Wire left, where Ben Jones-Bishop tried to claim the ball in the air but knocked on. Soon after the resulting scrum Wire opened the scoring, Myler ghosting through a gap after three minutes to give us the dream start.

For the next few minutes Warrington continue to be in the ascendancy and despite my love of sporting drama I am hoping for a runaway Wire victory. A knock-on from Waterhouse on his own 30-metre line after eight minutes or so allows Leeds to get a bit of a foothold in the game for the first time, then as the darkness falls the vampires start to take over. First of all they force a drop-out after Riley docs well to catch a high kick but is just about trapped in goal. Then they have a try chalked off when a borderline call goes against them, Sinfield's long pass to Hall being judged forward.

After 15 minutes Briers creates a break to provide some respite for Wire. His long cut-out pass puts Joel Monaghan in the clear on the last tackle, he races down the touchline then kicks the ball back inside towards the posts. The ball hits the ground and could have gone anywhere, but it falls into the grateful arms of Sinfield. Had it have gone to a Wire player and allowed them to stroll in then Wire would have had a 12-point lead.

Within a couple of minutes it's Sinfield who is launching the high kick, aiming for it to come down close to the Wire line. Monaghan and Hall contest the ball in the air, it bounces off Monaghan's arms and once again it could have gone anywhere, but once again it ended up in the arms of a Leeds player, this time Ablett. Sinfield has followed his own kick and a quick offload from Ablett allows Sinfield to stretch out and score in the corner, then the inevitable successful conversion ties the scores at 6-6.

Leeds continue in the ascendency, helped by the occasional handling error and penalty from Wire. The penalty that gives them an 8-6 lead is one of those that even some ardent Leeds fan would have to put in the 'harsh' category, Harrison penalised for interfering at the play-the-ball when as he is getting to his feet his knee brushes the ball. After another penalty Leeds are attacking about ten metres away from the Warrington try-line and McGuire flings out an accurate pass to Ben Jones-Bishop who catches the ball and steps inside in one motion, completely outfoxing his marker Riley and then the covering Hodgson to crash over and give Leeds a 14-6 lead.

Just when it looked like it might turn out to be Leeds who ran away with it, Wire's desire to defend kept them in the game. An eight-point deficit was wiped out in the space of a few minutes just before half-time. Briers showed great nerve as well as skill to fling out a fantastic long, left-handed pass to allow Joel Monaghan a stroll over the line. Another foray on the Leeds line resulted in a penalty just before half-time that allowed Hodgson to level the scores. Then we had the inspiring but almost comical sight of both teams running off the pitch at the same time, each desperate to show to the other that they were more of a team by being the ones that got off the pitch together first. Wire won that particular battle, but only because they were nearer the tunnel to start with.

So the entire championship campaign came down to the last 40 minutes. Anybody who still thinks that psychology doesn't play a big part in the outcome of sporting contests should watch these two teams play at Wembley and then at Old Trafford. Here Leeds couldn't feel more comfortable, whereas Wembley is far out of their comfort zone, Wire are the other way round. Warrington far from froze on the big occasion, but there did look to be a little bit of stage fright about their performance. From my vantage point it looked as if Leeds edged the battle down the middle, they were doing all the ugly things better, those things that help win the speed of the play-the-ball battle, a victory that so often results in winning the war.

Despite this Wire still found a way to be four points in front with around 20 minutes left after Atkins did exceptionally well to score in the corner. A play-the-ball less than five metres from Wire's left touchline meant it looked for all the world that Warrington would move the ball right but Hodgson had another idea. Realising Atkins and Riley were still on his left Hodgson jumped left with the ball before producing a little pop pass to Atkins. Watkins of Leeds was in position to tackle his opposite number, but maybe he was caught unaware by Hodgson tearing up the rule book. Watkins didn't move forwards to meet Atkins at all and trying to stop Atkins while standing still is a bit like trying to stop a runaway train with some traffic cones.

Two minutes after Atkins' try Michael Monaghan makes a break down our right. Crossing the halfway line, his pass to Ratchford is tantalisingly close to being caught but results in a knock-on. Maybe that was our moment to take control, but in a match of so many big moments it was hard to pick out one as a turning point. Maybe looking for a big turning point was one of the things that cost Wire. A couple of inventive last tackle options by Briers don't really come off, and a floated crossfield kick in his own half isn't quite gathered in by Joel Monaghan. Then a few minutes later dummying to kick and then looking for an inside ball to Hill doesn't come off the way Briers had hoped either.

It was in these last 20 minutes that the difference between the champions and the challengers became most apparent. A sustained spell of pressure from Leeds brought about the almost inevitable try, Ablett crashing over and Sinfield's subsequent conversion giving them a vital two-point lead. Five minutes later in an incident remarkably similar to one at Wembley, Leuluai smashes a Wire player in possession. At Wembley it was Hodgson and here it was Higham. Once again the Wire player loses the ball as a result of Leuluai's force, once again the tackle is judged legal, this once looks a lot more of a foul than the Wembley one to me as the arm is swung into the face of Higham after glancing contact with his chest. Warrington manage to survive that loss of possession, but really could have done with that penalty.

Not long afterwards Warrington get the break they desperately need, Delaney getting a fingertip to a Waterhouse pass, resulting in a knock-on and allowing Wire to start a set on the halfway line. Warrington's spirit was far from broken and they did advance the ball within ten metres of the Leeds line, then Chris Hill had the ball stripped from him and when he gathered it up again Wire had a new set of six tackles, ten metres from the Leeds line with 12 minutes left. The crowd roared as they sensed the potential of a winning score.

After all that exhausting fitness work in pre-season and throughout the year, all the tries scored, tackles made, games won, drawn and lost, humiliations in France, Salford and London, surviving a Biblical downpour to win at Wembley, proving they can win in the play-offs when it really mattered, after all that Wire had this one moment to seize the ultimate glory and end the 57-year wait.

From around 200 rows back the players didn't seem to get my signal to calm down. Earlier Leeds had showed all the composure needed to grind out a try that put them in the lead. Just when they needed it most, Wire's composure deserted them, and for a few crazy moments they seemed to play with the giddiness of a bunch of kids in the park who had just heard the call that their tea was ready and they had to come in at the end of the next play. The ball was knocked forward and the moment to seize the championship had gone. Wire had earned the right to have that opportunity to wrest the title from Leeds' grasp, but in a fleeting moment that opportunity had slipped out of their hands.

They needed the sort of composure that Rob Burrow showed in the semi-final against Wigan, when in the dying minutes, with his team one point behind, he found himself at acting half-back after a crucial error from Wigan. He could have easily flung out a wild pass or tried to find a way through the retreating Wigan defence for a try but instead he picked up the ball and made a beeline for an offside Wigan player, inviting the tackle and earning the penalty that allowed Sinfield to kick Leeds to Old Trafford once again.

Sport at the elite level can be so brutal. Leeds were in no mood to give Wire another chance and they had more than enough experience to show how to win the big game from there. They produced an off-the-cuff handling move of their own that resulted in lots of space for Ablett to create the match-clinching try for Ryan Hall.

Final score: Wire 18 Leeds 26

AFTER THE semi-finals I likened the Leeds team to vampires, due to them seemingly always playing better in the dark of night. When a vampire bites you they kill you or turn you into a vampire, so here's hoping this Wire team are far from dead.

Of course it was a disappointing way to end the season. We finally thought it was our year and the more you want something the more it hurts when you don't get it. One can only imagine how crushed the players feel, after putting their bodies on the line all year and putting their hearts and souls into winning the ultimate prize. Paul Wood's injury, that is not at all suitable reading for the squeamish, is in a way a fitting injury for this team as whatever else you can say about them this team have shown plenty of balls.

Let us not forget where we were four years ago. Could we have imagined then being devastated at the end of a season that has seen a Challenge Cup win, a second-placed finish in the league and a Grand Final appearance? Fans of other teams might well be laughing at us for losing in the Grand Final, but they used to just laugh at us in general. So while we might not be the ones laughing last this time, we certainly have plenty of things to smile about. We are getting nearer. The last four years have been a heck of a ride, let's hope the journey is just beginning.

Back in 2009 I wrote that open letter to the players questioning their sense of duty and commitment. In it I wrote: "I am reminded of a quote from Grantland Rice, an old American sportswriter: 'For when the One Great Scorer comes to write against your name, He marks – not that you won or lost – But how you played the game.' Fans just want to see you being as passionate about their team as they are."

I doubt many if any of the players read my humble articles, but if any of you do I would like to thank you for living up to the spirit of the letter and that quote in particular. Take a few weeks off to recover from the season and take a few moments to congratulate yourself on giving this town a team they can be proud of.

Then keep reminding yourself of another part of that letter: "The fact that you have been born with the required physical attributes to play professional rugby league, grown up in an area that allowed you to play the game, been spotted by a talent scout and managed to avoid career ending injuries, doesn't make you better than the fans, it makes you luckier than the fans."

Thanks for four fantastic seasons fellas but the holy grail is still out there waiting to be grabbed. You are lucky enough to go in search of it yourself. Some of us have to settle for writing about it.

For more details on my other books and writing and to leave comments, please check out the following websites:
https://sites.google.com/site/robwatsonbooks/home
https://www.facebook.com/LupineRobsbooks